the CALIFORNIA FARM TABLE COOKBOOK

the CALIFORNIA FARM TABLE COOKBOOK

100 Recipes from the Golden State

LORI RICE

Countryman Press

An Imprint of W. W. Norton & Company
Independent Publishers Since 1923

For information about permission to reproduce selections
from this book, write to Permissions, Countryman Press,
500 Fifth Avenue, New York, NY 10110

For information about special discounts for bulk
purchases, please contact W. W. Norton Special Sales at
specialsales@wwnorton.com or 800-233-4830

Manufacturing by Toppan Leefung Pte. Ltd.
Production manager: Devon Zahn

Countryman Press
www.countrymanpress.com

An imprint of W. W. Norton & Company, Inc.
500 Fifth Avenue, New York, NY 10110
www.wwnorton.com

978-1-68268-865-6

10 9 8 7 6 5 4 3 2 1

To my husband, who listened to me when I said I'm ready to turn our lives upside down. Thank you for moving to California with me and for all the adventures since.

To my parents, for passing on a love of farm-to-table before it was cool. I'm pretty sure I broke your hearts when I moved to the West Coast, but I'm forever grateful that I've been able to become the person I was meant to be.

CONTENTS

CHAPTER 3. FROM THE PASTURE

CHAPTER 4. FROM THE WATER

CHAPTER 5. AT THE TABLE

INTRODUCTION

When my husband and I moved to California in 2012, I brought with me my insatiable desire to see where food comes from. My curiosity for knowing the origins of our food and drink are even stronger than my interest in exploring those ingredients in the kitchen. I quickly learned that there was no better place for someone like me to land.

The journey began in the Bay Area and living within walking distance to what I still consider the best farmers' markets in the country. It was followed by five years in the Central Valley with walnut and orange trees around every corner. Now, on the Central Coast, I get to immerse myself in a top wine region while exploring the foods that we pull from our waters and those that are nurtured on the expansive land of our ranches.

The beauty of and accessibility to the foods and drinks we have here will never be lost on me. Quite frankly, I don't think I'll ever get over it. In December, I browse farmers' market aisles with a skip in my step, asking vendors the names of blood orange varieties. I pull my car off on the side of the road to capture photos of pomegranates and persimmons in the fall. I stop to marvel at trees loaded with lemons during neighborhood walks in late summer.

I say all this to tell you that what you hold in your hands is the culmination of everything I am passionate about. A dream project, if you will. Writing and photographing this book gave me the opportunity to dive more deeply in to my research of California's limitless array of fruits, vegetables, dairy, meats, and seafood as well as wine, beer, and spirits. I traveled to each of the farms and producers you'll read about, where I learned why they do what they do and how much they value bringing us these things we get to eat and drink. Then, I was able to create recipes using these ingredients as well as share a few from others.

Although I thoroughly enjoyed writing my last two books, *Food on Tap* and *Beer Bread*, where I incorporated craft beers into cooking and baking, in those books, these fresh ingredients I have all around me were things I simply integrated. In this book, they get to be the star. I had all the freedom to celebrate the avocados, artichokes, dates, garlic, figs, grass-fed beef, Dungeness crab, and oysters that California is known for, and so much more.

As you turn the pages, I hope you savor this journey through the foods and drinks that we are so fortunate to have at our doorsteps, and that many people also get to enjoy around the country. I hope you find the stories of these food and drink producers as inspiring as I did. Finally, I hope you are encouraged to pick a recipe, find an avocado, a fig, or another local ingredient, and celebrate California at your own table.

ABOUT CALIFORNIA AND THIS COOKBOOK

California's Food and Drink, and the People Who Grow and Make It

California is known for food. People hear about our food, our chefs, and our restaurants all the time, whether on cooking reality shows, at major culinary award ceremonies, or through a viral magazine article. California has a food scene, and it's not just in the major cities. Our small towns are full of hidden gems that span from celebrated local dives to Michelin-starred establishments.

It's what is behind this food scene that may go unnoticed. You can't make an award-winning meal without the best ingredients. What we really have in California are the best ingredients. Ingredients grown and produced by local family farms, large and small, with decades of history and diversity that are unmatched.

California is home to farms, orchards, and ranches rooted in Japanese, German, Italian, and Latin American cultures. We have sixth-generation fruit orchards still operating. We have farms that incorporate African Indigenous agroecology and those applying ancient Jewish values to how they grow and share food.

There are food producers here who have grown food their entire lives, those who left and came back to the farm, and those who switched careers to make the production of food and drink their life's work. In the back of this book, you'll find the websites of the people you read about here. I highly suggest taking a look and reading their histories. There is so much more to each of these farms, food makers, and drink producers than can be covered in one book.

California grows one-third of the country's vegetables and three-quarters of its fruits and nuts. While almonds, oranges, grapes, walnuts, and strawberries are some of our top crops, these don't even scratch the surface of what is truly available in this great state. Artichokes, avocados, carrots, dates, figs, garlic, kiwifruit, olives, pistachios, and rice are a few more of the surprises uncovered once you start exploring.

Then there are all the varieties within each of these foods that are regularly spotted at farmers' markets throughout the state. Some even make it out of the state, allowing others to experience our good culinary fortune. There are the velvety pink heads of Radicchio Rosa; yellow and green–striped Panache Tiger figs; creamy, caramel-like Honey dates; and Sevillano olives grown for table olives that also produce a delicate, herbaceous oil.

Unbeknownst to many who don't live here, our foods in California do have seasons. Be ready for boxes overflowing with blood oranges, mandarins, and tangerines from December to early spring. Keep an eye out for heirloom baby artichokes in March. Fresh figs will start in early June with Mission and Brown Turkey figs pushing through fall. But those Tiger figs last only a few weeks in late summer.

Everything grown in California is worth looking forward to, but if you want those rarer varieties that make it even more exciting to live here, be ready to cook and eat seasonally just as other parts of the country do. This book is here to help you do that.

Inside This Book

Within these chapters, you will find stories about those who grow and produce food and drinks, and those who bridge the gap between grower and table with their culinary creations.

Surrounding these stories are recipes celebrating the foods and drinks of California. Some are from me, inspired by both my farm-to-table upbringing and my time spent exploring this state. Others are from chefs and restaurants that pride themselves on using local ingredients. Some of the featured farms have also trusted me with longtime family recipes that I'm honored to share with you here on these pages.

Within each chapter, there are recipes focusing on the foods that thrive in our soils and hang in our trees, those food sources that roam our pastures, and those that are gathered from our waters. With temperate climates throughout much of the state, California is also known for bringing things to the table for gatherings from spring brunch to autumn dinner parties. You'll find suggestions for hosting your own using the farm table recipes shared inside.

A side note on terminology: I've done my best to research and use accurate terms to describe the foods, drinks, and those who produce them in this book. The one thing I stumbled on the most was the term used for those who catch the fish and seafood from our waters. After speaking to people on all sides of the industry from those doing the fishing, to those marketing it and researching it, I've applied what I've learned to the words you'll read here. While *fishers* is used in academic writing, the most widely used term in all other applications, and one that is used and supported by those fishing regardless of gender identification, is *fishermen*.

Cooking and Baking the Recipes in This Book

The recipes you'll find among these pages highlight California ingredients with instructions tailored to your success in making them. While each is formatted to be similar for consistency, there are recipes created by me in this book and those provided to me by others.

We all cook a little differently, with brands and ingredients we trust and always turn to. You will find suggestions for some of the products made by those featured in this book and I encourage you to seek them out. Even if you don't live in the state, many of our producers ship what they make and grow. If you can't find them, I've done my best to suggest something similar, if it exists, but some ingredients may be essential to the recipes.

Before you get started, there are basic ingredients, tools, and topics I'd like to address.

Dairy

This book celebrates the rich creams, milks, cheeses, and yogurts that are produced here in California. While many of our local producers do make low-fat and nonfat products, this book does not use them. You'll find whole milk, heavy cream, and full-fat yogurts in the ingredient lists. These hearty dairy products are what make the recipes that use them exceptional, so I encourage you to choose full-fat.

Flour

Whether you live in California or not, look beyond the supermarket shelves for flour. Most areas of the country have small flour mills making a farm-to-table effort at delivering heirloom grains for us to use in our baking. Many recipes in the book use all-purpose flour, but such varieties as hard red spring wheat and white spring wheat are used, too. Use these recipes as an opportunity to seek out local flours in your area or to buy from the producers featured in this book.

If you do have trouble finding heirloom flours, the following are some general definitions for those often found on store shelves in case you need to make substitutions. Brands can vary, so be sure to do your own research. For the best results, always use the weight measurement for flour provided in each baking recipe.

STONE-GROUND WHOLE WHEAT FLOUR: made from hard red wheat
WHITE WHOLE WHEAT FLOUR: made from hard white wheat
PASTRY FLOUR: made from soft white or soft red wheat
ALL-PURPOSE FLOUR: a blend of hard and soft wheat

Olive Oil

We are fortunate to have some of the best olive oil in the world available at farmers' markets and at our local specialty stores. These small producers create oils with flavors some may have never experienced. They can be peppery, grassy, earthy, smooth, acidic, and creamy. You can cook with these oils and use them to finish a salad or pizza. You'll find my suggestions in some recipes for the type of oil to use in terms of flavor profiles. Use these suggestions as an opportunity to explore the large varieties of olive oils grown and pressed in California.

Salt and Seasonings

I'm notorious, if only to myself, for undersalting. This is simply because I'm not a chef, but a nutritional scientist and cook, which has prompted me to always use a reserved hand with the salt jar. It's resolved itself over the years as I've worked with more chefs, translating, and testing their recipes. So, I think we're safe now.

You'll find that I give exact measurements for salt. I think that's important when making someone else's recipe. But I also include the option to add more salt to taste, if desired. We all have different salt tolerances, and while some people argue that you shouldn't leave it up to taste, I feel that you most certainly should.

I use fine sea salt in my cooking and baking, but standard table salt can be substituted. Some of the recipes provided by chefs and farms specify kosher salt, while others simply list salt—use table salt for these. When it comes to finishing salts, be sure to seek out a bold, naturally made sea salt like that from the producer in this book (page 224).. California has some exceptional sea salts.

I suggest crushed Aleppo chile pepper a lot in this book. I discovered it a few years back and really fell for its fruity heat. It's widely available online, but if you'd rather not keep it on hand, I've noted in most recipes that you can substitute crushed red pepper flakes. Except for in Cracked Dungeness Crab with Garlic Sea Salt and Aleppo Pepper (page 196). It really is a key ingredient in the flavors of this dish.

Shopping for Your Produce

To make your farmers' market and farm stand shopping easier, you will find ingredient lists that include fruits and vegetables in market measurements, such as the number of fruit or the weight of the vegetables. Don't fret too much over exact sizes. If your garlic clove or shallot is a little bigger than mine, it's only going to add more flavor to the final dish. If the exact amount prepared is important for a successful result, I've also included ingredients in cups or similar measurements. For very small amounts, such as 1 tablespoon of onions or herbs, measurements are typically in tablespoons and teaspoons.

Kitchen Tools

Nothing out of the ordinary is needed for the majority of recipes in this book. There are a few exceptions, so read through the instructions before you jump in. A kitchen scale is strongly suggested for baked recipes and is essential if you plan to make California Whole Wheat Sourdough (page 79). You will also need a Dutch oven or cast-iron cooker and ideally a proofing basket for that recipe. A Dutch oven is also helpful for the roasted meats in Chapter 3. I also use a mandoline to thinly slice produce in some recipes, but if you are skilled with a knife, you can do this by hand.

Otherwise, standard tools, such as a blender, hand or stand mixer, and everyday assorted baking dishes, pots, saucepans, and baking sheets, are all you need. For recipes that I exclusively use a cast-iron skillet to make, I have pointed that out.

It may seem like an unimportant thing to mention, but I always roast and bake with brown parchment paper. It's not required, but for years I thought it was only to protect your pan for easy cleanup. It turns out that things roast and bake much more beautifully and evenly when I use it, so it is now a staple in my kitchen.

It doesn't take much to guarantee your success with this cookbook. Just gather up all your California ingredients and head to the kitchen.

CHAPTER 1

FROM THE SOIL

One of my favorite drives through the state is the section of Highway 101 that extends from the Bay Area down to the Central Coast. It's the best route for getting a glimpse of the color that bursts from California soils. Row crops of green and purple lettuce create a watercolor painting on the roadside. Heads of broccoli and leaves of kale sit atop crumbles of brown soil in the Salinas Valley. If you turn off the beaten path, the vegetation gets taller and soon you are among leafy green plants topped with artichokes reaching toward the sunshine.

While this area is a good place to start for witnessing our soil crops, it certainly isn't where it ends. Both large and small farms grow row and field crops in nearly every part of the state. Strawberries, lettuce, tomatoes, rice, carrots, and broccoli are in the top 20 of the foods grown here. Artichokes, cabbage, eggplants, garlic, grapes, kale, melons, onions, and peppers are a few of the other foods we lead the nation in growing, thanks to our farmers.

There are also crops that help create the drinks for pairing with all these foods. Grain growers aid in producing ingredients that supply our craft breweries and distilleries. With thousands of wineries in the state, you can't drive far in any direction before the landscape turns from fields of leafy greens to vines of chardonnay and zinfandel.

While each of the chapters in this book blends several California ingredients, in this one you'll find recipes that highlight the plants rooted in our soils and the foods we pull from it.

Steamed Globe Artichokes with White Wine Dijon Sauce

SERVES 4

I had no idea how to eat a steamed artichoke until I moved to California. If you are unfamiliar, too, it's supersimple. Once you steam the artichoke, the leaves will easily pull off. You'll notice that the bottom is a bit thicker with a white flesh. Pop that end in your mouth and use your teeth to scrape off the tender meat. Before you do, though, give the fleshy bottom of the leaf a dip in a sauce, such as the tangy, savory option in this recipe. I like to use a mellow chardonnay with a hint of citrus that's a little on the creamy, buttery side.

Artichokes

3 garlic cloves, peeled

2 large globe artichokes

White Wine Dijon Sauce

2 tablespoons salted butter

1 tablespoon minced shallot

1 garlic clove, minced

1 tablespoon Dijon mustard

1 teaspoon spicy brown mustard

¼ cup chicken stock

¼ cup white wine, such as chardonnay

Pinch of fine sea salt, or to taste

1. Make the artichokes: Fill the bottom basin of a steamer pot about one-third full of water, ensuring that the water line doesn't reach the steamer basket. Drop the garlic cloves into the water. Add the lid and bring the water to a boil over medium-high heat.

2. Remove a layer of leaves at the bottom of each artichoke and trim the stem to about ½ inch. Cut the top third off each artichoke, then use scissors to trim away the pointed ends of all the remaining leaves.

3. Place the artichokes upside down in a steamer basket so that the stem end is up. Lower the heat beneath the water to a simmer and place the basket over the water. Secure the lid and steam the artichokes until the leaves are tender and pull off easily, about 45 minutes.

4. While the artichokes steam, make the sauce: Melt the butter in a small saucepan. Stir in the shallot and garlic and cook for 2 minutes, stirring often to prevent them from browning.

5. Whisk in the mustards, then the chicken stock. Lower the heat to low and carefully stir in the wine. Return the heat to medium-high and bring the sauce to a boil. Boil for 5 minutes, stirring occasionally. Adjust the heat as needed during cooking to prevent the sauce from boiling over. The sauce will thicken slightly and reduce by about half. Remove from the heat, stir in the salt, and let cool.

6. Once the artichokes are tender, serve warm on a platter with the room-temperature dipping sauce on the side.

PEZZINI FARMS

SEAN PEZZINI, CASTROVILLE

Sean Pezzini's great-grandfather started growing artichokes in 1920 on the same land that Sean farms today. While others were buying up land a little farther north in Monterey and Carmel, it soon became clear that this spot in California, about 2 miles from the ocean with fertile soils, was perfect for artichokes. They thrive in the cool coastal climate and the dark, rich soil that was once wetlands. In fact, the city has been called the Artichoke Capital of the World.

"What makes our artichokes different is that we are growing heirloom artichokes," says Sean. He explains that these artichokes are grown as a perennial, so the rootstock stays in the ground year after year. "It's pretty much the same rootstock that my great-grandpa was farming one hundred years ago," he says. "It's considered an heirloom because it's been passed down through the generations."

The area used to be home to tens of thousands of acres of heirloom artichokes, but many farmers have gotten away from producing them because they are so labor intensive. While what are called seeded artichokes that you find in the supermarket are grown here, only a few farms still grow these heirloom artichokes, so they can be hard to find. When you get your hands on some, you will undoubtedly be able to tell the difference.

Sean describes the heirlooms as meaty, nutty, and often sweet. How and what you cook with them influences the artichoke as well. Larger artichokes are best steamed, and Sean suggests steaming them upside down so that the steam can get into the layers of leaves.

A special thing about these heirloom plants is that they produce baby artichokes farther down

on the stalk, something you often don't find in stores. These small artichokes get less sunlight and nutrients than the larger ones at the top of the plant, so they stay small, and they can be easier to tackle in the kitchen. Once you peel off the outer green leaves, you can steam or sauté to cook them and then eat the entire thing.

It's true that fresh artichokes take some time to prepare and cook, but I like the way Sean looks at it. "I compare it to a specialty like Dungeness crab. It's a lot of work to get to that little bit of meat, but when you get to it, it's worth it," he says.

Baby Artichokes with Sun-Dried Tomatoes, Capers, and Garlic

SERVES 4

Since Sean Pezzini introduced me to heirloom baby artichokes, I haven't looked back. I still love the occasional steamed large artichoke, but when it comes to easy prep and the option to add lots of flavor, I choose the baby variety every time. These tender artichokes get a pleasant salinity from the capers that's balanced by a sweet tanginess from sun-dried tomatoes. It's a simple side dish for grilled meats or broiled fish, but it also makes a special topping for your tagliatelle on pasta night.

Juice of 1 lemon (2 tablespoons)

12 baby artichokes (1¼ pounds)

2 tablespoons extra-virgin olive oil

2 garlic cloves, minced

2 tablespoons sliced oil-packed sun-dried tomatoes

1 tablespoon chopped capers

¼ teaspoon fine sea salt, or to taste

¼ teaspoon ground black pepper, or to taste

1. Add the lemon juice to a shallow bowl before you start cleaning the artichokes.

2. Working one artichoke at a time, peel the outer leaves from the artichoke until you are left with a small, arrow-shaped bulb that is creamy yellow at the bottom and green only at the very top. Trim the top third of the artichoke to remove the remaining tough, bright green parts. Then, use a paring knife to peel the short stem and trim the stem end.

3. Cut the artichoke in half lengthwise and place it in the lemon juice to slow the browning as you work. Repeat for each artichoke.

4. Heat the olive oil in a large skillet with a lid over medium-high. Transfer the artichokes to the oil and pour in the lemon juice they were soaking in. Stir and cook for 2 minutes.

5. Arrange each half so it is cut side down. Lower the heat to medium and cover with the lid. Let cook for 3 minutes, or until the cut sides are browned. When you remove the lid, you'll be hit with a pleasant green artichoke aroma. Stir and lower the heat to medium-low.

6. Add the garlic and stir often to prevent it from burning. Lower the heat if needed. Cook the artichokes until they are fork-tender, 2 to 3 more minutes.

7. Turn off the heat and stir in the sun-dried tomatoes, with their oil, and the capers. Add the salt and pepper. Stir well. Serve warm.

Simple Garlic Soup

SERVES 4 AS A STARTER

Gilroy, California, is known as the Garlic Capital of the World and this soup highlights one of our most plentiful crops. It's full of caramelized, roasted garlic for a savory starter that is creamier than a broth, but not so thick that it's too heavy and filling. Plan ahead with this one because you'll need to roast the garlic for 45 minutes. I like to throw the heads in any time I have the oven going for other things, so that the garlic is ready to go when I want to make the soup. The roasted cloves can be stored in the refrigerator for up to three days. The soup is topped with homemade sourdough croutons, but your favorite store-bought croutons or crackers make a nice addition for serving, too.

4 heads garlic

2 tablespoons plus 2 teaspoons extra-virgin olive oil

4 cups chicken stock

One 3-inch thyme sprig

2 teaspoons cornstarch

2 teaspoons water

¼ cup whole milk

1 ounce Parmesan, finely grated (about ⅓ cup)

¾ teaspoon fine sea salt, or to taste

⅛ teaspoon ground black pepper

Fresh thyme for garnish

Croutons

1 cup cubed sourdough bread (¼-inch cubes)

1 tablespoon extra-virgin olive oil

¼ teaspoon fine sea salt

¼ teaspoon garlic powder

¼ teaspoon ground black pepper

¼ teaspoon dried thyme

1. Preheat the oven to 400°F.

2. Cut the top quarter off each head of garlic, to expose each clove. Place each head on a square of aluminum foil large enough to wrap the garlic. Divide the 2 teaspoons of olive oil equally over each head. Wrap the foil around each head.

3. Place the garlic in the oven and roast for 45 minutes, or until completely softened. Remove from the oven, carefully open the foil, and let them sit until cool enough to handle, about 10 minutes.

4. While the garlic roasts, you can make the croutons: Toss the bread cubes in the olive oil on a baking sheet and sprinkle with the salt, garlic powder, pepper, and thyme. Spread in a single layer and bake for 3 minutes, then stir and bake for another 5 minutes, or until golden brown. Remove from the oven and set aside to cool.

5. Squeeze the roasted garlic cloves from the heads into a bowl. Discard the skins. Use a fork or clean hands to smash the cloves. Remove any skins or hard parts of the head that may have dropped in while squeezing in the cloves.

6. Heat the remaining 2 tablespoons of olive oil in a small soup pot over medium-high. Stir in the garlic and cook until fragrant, 1 minute. Pour in the stock and add the thyme sprig. Bring the soup to a boil and then boil for 5 minutes. Remove and discard the thyme stem.

7. Stir together the cornstarch and water in a small bowl. Lower the heat to medium-low and whisk in the cornstarch slurry. Whisk in the milk and increase the heat to medium. Continue to whisk as the soup comes back to a simmer; continue to whisk and let the soup thicken for 5 more minutes.

8. Turn off the heat and stir in the Parmesan, salt, and pepper. Garnish with fresh thyme leaves and serve warm with croutons.

Green Garlic Buttermilk Biscuits

MAKES 5 BISCUITS

Green garlic is what results when you harvest garlic early before it becomes the bulb and segmented cloves that most of us are familiar with. When picked, it looks more like a spring onion or a small leek. It's the aroma that gives it away. While the smell confirms it is garlic, its flavor is milder than a mature head of the allium. In this recipe, the green garlic is cooked in olive oil until nearly crisp and then it's baked into buttermilk biscuits. If you don't have green garlic, you can make these using scallions or leeks. They won't have quite the same flavor, but you'll still end up with a craveable biscuit.

½ teaspoon extra-virgin olive oil

2 green garlic stalks, minced

1 teaspoon fine sea salt

2 cups (240 g) all-purpose flour,
    plus more for dusting

1½ teaspoons baking powder

½ teaspoon ground black pepper

8 tablespoons (1 stick) cold unsalted butter, cubed

¾ cup (6 ounces) buttermilk, plus more as needed

1 large egg

1 tablespoon water

Note: Trim the root ends of the garlic and use the white portion through the light green portion for this recipe. It's usually about 4 inches of the stalk. You'll need ¼ cup minced, which is about two small stalks.

1. Heat the olive oil in a small skillet over medium-high. Lower the heat to medium and add the garlic. Cook, stirring constantly to prevent the garlic from burning, until the pieces are browned with some crispy, about 2 minutes. Remove from the heat and stir in ¼ teaspoon of the salt. Transfer to a paper towel–covered plate to absorb any excess oil.

2. Preheat the oven to 425°F. Line a baking sheet with parchment paper.

3. Combine the flour, baking powder, the remaining ¾ teaspoon of salt, and the pepper in a medium bowl. Stir to mix, then stir in the green garlic.

4. Add the butter and use two knives or a pastry blender to work the butter into the flour until it is evenly distributed in pea-size pieces. Add the buttermilk a little at a time, and stir or knead into a dough ball. It should be soft and slightly sticky but firm enough to handle and shape. Add a little less or a little more buttermilk, if needed, to reach the right consistency.

5. Lightly dust the dough ball with flour and place on a floured surface. Pat it out to a disk about ¾ inch thick or about 7 inches in diameter. Use a 3-inch round biscuit cutter to cut five biscuits. You will need to combine and reshape the scraps. A different size cutter can be used. In that case, your number of total biscuits and exact baking time will vary.

6. Place the biscuits at least 1 inch apart on the prepared baking sheet. Stir together the egg and water in a small bowl to create an egg wash. Brush the tops and sides of the biscuits with the egg wash. Discard any extra you don't use.

7. Bake the biscuits for 22 minutes, or until golden brown and no longer doughy in the center. Enjoy warm or at room temperature.

J. MARCHINI FARMS

FRANCESCA MARCHINI FORDICE, LE GRAND

If you've ever enjoyed US-grown radicchio, you have the Marchini family to thank for it. Their farming journey began in the 1920s in Le Grand, California, when Francesca Marchini Fordice's great-grandfather arrived from Lucca, Italy, and began growing tomatoes. By the 1980s, her grandfather Joe Marchini began experimenting with seeds from Italy, and he soon became the original radicchio grower in the United States. Due to his perseverance in introducing people in California to the leafy vegetable, heads of radicchio can now be found in supermarkets and at farmers' markets, and its deep burgundy leaves are mixed into bagged salads found around the country.

Today, the family grows round heads of Radicchio di Chioggia, the oblong Treviso, cream-colored and pink-speckled Castelfranco, and light pink Radicchio Rosa in addition to lacinato kale, fennel, frisée, Italian specialties such as Cardone and Puntarelle, and fresh figs. They distribute nationwide under the brand name Joe's Premium. They also supply California chefs and sell at Fresno-area farmers' markets.

On their true family farm, Francesca's father, Jeff, and her brother Nic work in farming operations while her brother Marc works in sales and postharvest operations. Francesca now works in sales and marketing, making connections with

local restaurants and farmers' markets exploring new ways to get what they grow into the hands of consumers.

"All my life I knew that growing food, especially healthy food, was the one thing that always grounded me," says Francesca. While growing up, it was the norm in her life that everyone worked in agriculture, but as an adult, confirmation of the importance of what she and her family do has only gotten stronger. "We're farmers. And we're proud to be farmers. We're not going anywhere. We want to keep farming because being a farmer, you connect with people on so many levels," she says.

Radicchio Pasta Salad

SERVES 6 TO 8

This colorful pasta salad comes from J. Marchini Farms and perfectly highlights the touch of bitterness and tender bite of its beautiful radicchio. I like to make this in late January, when all varieties that they grow are in season, so I took the liberty of not only adding the round, purple Radicchio di Chioggia many of us are familiar with, but also Treviso, Radicchio Rosa, and Castelfranco. The mix gives this recipe an explosion of color to go along with its blend of bold flavors.

1 pound orzo pasta, cooked and cooled

⅔ cup oil-packed sun-dried tomatoes, chopped

⅔ cup pitted Kalamata olives, chopped

1 cup pine nuts, toasted

1 head radicchio, sliced

1½ cups baby arugula

1 small red onion, sliced

1 cup fresh basil, torn

1 cup freshly grated Parmigiana-Reggiano

6 tablespoons extra-virgin olive oil

6 tablespoons balsamic vinegar

½ teaspoon kosher salt, or to taste

¼ teaspoon ground black pepper, or to taste

1. Place the orzo in a large bowl. Add the sun-dried tomatoes, olives, pine nuts, radicchio, arugula, onion, and basil. Stir gently a few times.

2. Sprinkle in the cheese, and drizzle in the olive oil and balsamic vinegar. Stir well to combine all the ingredients. Add the salt and pepper. Taste and add more, if desired.

3. Serve immediately, or store in the fridge overnight and toss to mix before serving.

J. Marchini Farms

Endive Celery Salad with Creamy Garlic-Orange Dressing and Pistachios

SERVES 2 TO 4

Endive and celery may not be the first things we think of when naming foods associated with California, but they are two more vegetables the state leads the nation in growing. I bring them both together in this crunchy salad. The creamy dressing is just what the slightly bitter endive and the sweet crunch of the celery need, creating a harmony of flavors and textures. Any hard aged cheese, such as Parmesan, pairs well with this salad, but a more boldly flavored option, such as Pecorino Romano, is my first choice.

Garlic-Orange Dressing

3 tablespoons heavy whipping cream

2 tablespoons plain Greek yogurt

½ teaspoon honey

Zest of 1 small orange

1 tablespoon fresh orange juice

1 garlic clove, grated

¼ teaspoon fine sea salt

Pinch of ground black pepper

Endive Celery Salad

4 heads Belgian endive, sliced

2 celery stalks with leaves, diced

¼ cup roasted, salted pistachios, chopped

Grated aged hard cheese for serving

1. Make the dressing: Stir together the cream and yogurt in a small bowl. Add the honey and stir until it is dissolved into the dairy. Stir in the orange zest and juice, garlic, salt, and pepper until all the ingredients are combined. Set aside.

2. Make the salad: Toss together the endive and celery in a serving bowl or on a serving platter. Top with the pistachios and drizzle with as much dressing as desired. Top with grated cheese as desired and serve.

Sweet Rice with Fresh Strawberry Black Pepper Jam

SERVES 6

This dessert is a cross between sticky rice and rice pudding, two of my favorites. The sweetened, creamy rice is topped with a strawberry jam that has a lingering savory heat, thanks to black pepper and ginger. Strawberries are one of the top 10 crops grown in California, and they can be found nearly year-round at most farmers' markets. Those fresh berries are used to make the jam and then used to top each serving for an extra bit of juicy sweetness. If you don't have fresh nutmeg to grate, ground nutmeg is fine to use, but for the best flavor, stick with freshly ground or cracked black pepper from whole peppercorns.

Sweet Rice

1 cup uncooked short-grain, sweet rice

1 cup water

1¾ cups whole milk

3 tablespoons sugar

1 teaspoon pure vanilla extract

¼ teaspoon freshly grated nutmeg

Pinch of fine sea salt

Strawberry Jam

16 ounces strawberries, hulled and diced (3 cups)

¼ cup water

2 tablespoons sugar

¼ teaspoon freshly ground black pepper

¼ teaspoon ground ginger

¼ teaspoon pure vanilla extract

Note: I like to use Koda Farms' (page 43) Sho-Chiku-Bai sweet rice for this recipe. You can find sweet rice at most Asian or international markets and it's also widely available online.

1. Start the sweet rice: Place the rice in a bowl and cover with water. Let soak for 15 minutes.

2. While the rice soaks, make the jam: Reserve 1 cup of strawberries and add the remaining 2 cups to a medium saucepan. Add the water and sugar. Place over medium-high heat and bring to a boil.

3. Boil for 10 minutes, stirring often and smashing the berries as they cook. The strawberries will break down and the jam will reduce by half. Watch the jam closely as it boils, to ensure it doesn't boil over, continuing to stir often.

4. Remove the jam from the heat and stir in the pepper, ginger, and vanilla. Let cool for 5 minutes, then transfer to a bowl and let rest in the refrigerator while you make the rice.

5. Drain the soaking water from the rice and rinse the grains one more time. Add the cup of fresh water to a large saucepan and bring it to a boil over medium-high heat. Once the water is boiling, add the rice and stir constantly for 2 minutes. The water will absorb quickly.

6. Reserve ¼ cup of the milk. Lower the heat to medium and pour in the remaining 1½ cups of milk, ¼ cup at a time, as you continue to stir. Stir in the sugar. Continue to cook and stir until the rice is tender, 5 minutes.

7. Stir in the vanilla, nutmeg, and salt. Remove the saucepan from the heat. The rice will absorb more of the milk as it cools, so just before you are ready to transfer the rice to serving bowls, stir in the reserved ¼ cup of milk, or enough to reach a creamy but not soupy consistency.

8. Divide the rice among six bowls. Top with an equal amount of jam and then an equal amount of diced fresh berries. The rice can be served warm or at room temperature.

Roasted Balsamic Grape and Strawberry Salad

SERVES 4 TO 6

Grapes and berries are roasted with tangy balsamic vinegar to intensify their sweetness in this feast of a salad. The juices from roasting are used to make the dressing, then the whole meal comes together with crunchy California pistachios and creamy chèvre. It's filling on its own, but it also goes well with grilled chicken breasts or even leftover shredded rotisserie chicken.

Salad

1 pint strawberries, hulled and quartered (12 large berries)

1 large bunch small black or red seedless grapes (1½ cups)

1 tablespoon balsamic vinegar

1 tablespoon extra-virgin olive oil

¼ teaspoon fine sea salt

Pinch of ground black pepper

1 large head romaine lettuce

¾ cup roasted, salted pistachios

3 ounces chèvre, crumbled

Diced fresh strawberries and grapes for serving (optional)

Balsamic Dressing

1 tablespoon balsamic vinegar

1 tablespoon extra-virgin olive oil

½ teaspoon honey

¼ teaspoon fine sea salt

Pinch of ground black pepper

Notes: I like the crunch of a leafy head of romaine lettuce in this salad, but I do suggest using a full head for more flavor versus buying just the romaine hearts. Alternatively, you can substitute a spring mix. The fruit is roasted until soft, a texture that contrasts the crunchy romaine and provides juices for the dressing. If you prefer firmer fruit, you can reduce the roasting time by a few minutes or add more chopped fresh fruit to garnish the salad.

1. Start the salad: Preheat the oven to 425°F and line a baking sheet with parchment paper.

2. Spread the strawberries and grapes on the prepared pan. Drizzle with the balsamic vinegar and olive oil and then sprinkle with the salt and pepper. Stir and spread back into a single layer.

3. Roast for 10 minutes, stir, and then roast for another 5 minutes. The fruit will be soft and surrounded by juices.

4. Set a colander over a bowl and transfer the fruit to the colander to strain the juice. Pour any juices from the pan over the fruit. Let it all sit about 10 minutes, until the juice stops dripping into the bowl.

5. Pour the juices into a ½-pint mason jar. Return the fruit to the bowl to cool.

6. Make the dressing: Add the balsamic vinegar, olive oil, honey, salt, and pepper to the jar that contains the juices. Secure the lid and shake until combined, about 15 seconds.

7. Assemble the salad: Cut the romaine into large pieces and transfer to a serving platter. Top the lettuce with the fruit. Drizzle with the dressing, then add the pistachios and chèvre. Top with diced fresh strawberries and grapes, if desired. Serve right away.

TANAKA FARMS

GLENN, SHIRLEY, AND KENNY TANAKA, IRVINE

Farmer Glenn Tanaka is a sansei—a third-generation Japanese American—and farmer, who has been growing food for the Irvine area since the late 1970s. His knowledge of farming combined with his wife Shirley's background in food and nutrition has helped to make Tanaka Farms what it is today—a working farm and resource for community education that they own and operate with their son Kenny.

In 1998, when they moved to the 30 acres where they now farm in Irvine, they entered the agritourism space and were able to pursue their mission of showing others where food comes from. In addition to growing more than 65 crops, running a farm stand that sells their produce, and managing a Community-Supported Agriculture (CSA) subscription, they host hundreds of schools each year, enabling students to explore their fields of strawberries and their autumn pumpkin patch.

"What sets us apart is that we encourage people to try produce when they are at the farm," says Farmer Tanaka. Tours involve walking the field and tasting the produce right from the plant with the supervision of a host whom they call a Strawberry Lifeguard.

It's these tours and the education they do on the farm that drew Farmer Kenny, a yonsei, or fourth-generation Japanese American, to work at the farm. "We were having such a hard time; we didn't want him to be a farmer. But agritourism saved us," says Farmer Tanaka. The tours and opportunities to educate are what helped Farmer Kenny find his role working at the family farm.

The impact the tours have on visitors is something the family loves to see. "I take for granted being on the farm. When people come out, they don't need anything. It's enough for them just to taste and explore," says Farmer Tanaka.

Tanaka Farms Watermelon Poke Salad

SERVES 4 TO 6

Spring brings strawberry lovers to Tanaka Farms, but summers are all about bright, juicy watermelons. It's the time of year when team member and plant-based chef Joni Marie Newman makes her watermelon poke that she shares with us here. "This marinade will transform your watermelon from sweet to savory. Simmering the fruit softens it, making it the perfect substitute for ahi tuna in this vegan version of a poke salad," she says. The recipe also uses Maui onions grown on the farm. Another sweet variety of onion you have available can be substituted. You can eat this salad alone, on top of greens, or serve it over sticky rice.

Watermelon Poke

¼ cup unseasoned rice vinegar

2 tablespoons sesame oil

2 tablespoons soy sauce or tamari

1 tablespoon balsamic vinegar

**2 pounds cubed red seedless watermelon
(no larger than ½-inch cubes)**

Poke Salad

1 cup julienned Maui onions

1 cup chopped scallions

1 tablespoon sesame seeds

2 teaspoons soy sauce

Shredded nori for garnish

Toasted white or black sesame seeds for garnish

Lime wedges for serving

1. Make the watermelon poke: Combine the rice vinegar, sesame oil, soy sauce, balsamic vinegar, and cubed watermelon in a large pot with a lid. Stir well.

Cover with the lid and bring to a boil over medium-high heat. Lower the heat and simmer, covered, stirring occasionally, until the watermelon is tender and resembles the texture of raw tuna, about 30 minutes. Make sure there is no crunch left in the watermelon.

2. When the watermelon is tender, remove from the heat and strain off the excess liquid, leaving only the watermelon poke cubes. Place in a large bowl and chill in the refrigerator until you're ready to make the salad.

3. Make the poke salad: Add the Maui onions, scallions, sesame seeds, and soy sauce to the bowl of watermelon poke. Toss to combine all ingredients and coat the poke. Keep chilled until ready to serve.

4. When ready to serve, top with nori and sesame seeds and add lime wedges on the side for squeezing over the poke.

Joni Marie Newman for Tanaka Farms

Baby Fennel and Walnut Pesto

MAKES ABOUT 1 CUP

One thing that Jane Darrah (page 232) harvests among her microgreens is what is best described as baby fennel: small fronds that have just opened, providing a compact, yet wispy green that is bright with both earthiness and anise flavor. When she mentioned she thought it would be great in a pesto, I knew I needed to create one with the baby fronds she sent home with me. We used to make pesto at the bakery where I worked during high school and we always used walnuts for the creamiest texture imaginable. This is my twist on that pesto, using these microgreens. You can substitute the fronds of a fennel bulb, but the flavor may be bolder. Blending in some basil leaves can balance the boldness. One clove of garlic can be substituted for the scapes if they are out of season. I like to refrigerate the pesto about an hour before serving so that it's spreadable for toasted bread, or you can toss it with warm pasta.

1½ cups packed baby fennel fronds, chopped

2 ounces Parmesan, grated (⅔ cup)

1 small garlic scape, chopped

¼ cup raw walnut pieces

½ teaspoon fine sea salt

¼ teaspoon ground black pepper

¾ cup extra-virgin olive oil

1. Combine the fennel fronds, Parmesan, garlic scape, walnuts, salt, and pepper in a blender. Pulse about 10 times to begin chopping the ingredients.

2. Pour in half of the olive oil and puree on high speed for 15 seconds. Alternatively, you can pour the oil into the top chute of the blender while it is running, but I often find this makes a mess; adding it in two parts works better. Scrape the sides of the blender as needed.

3. Add the remaining olive oil and puree again for 15 seconds. I like my pesto with small yet visible pieces of nuts and herbs. For a smoother pesto, continue to puree until it reaches your preferred consistency. Refrigerate for about 1 hour before serving.

Carrot Noodle Salad

SERVES 4 TO 6

This chilled noodle salad is simple to make and a good choice for preparing a few hours ahead of serving, because the flavors only get better. I like to use lo mein noodles because they contain sodium that adds to the flavor of the dish. You can substitute another noodle, but just keep in mind that something like a rice noodle may need a little extra soy sauce to avoid a bland result. Sliced almonds, one of the top tree nuts grown in California, are my go-to here, but you can't go wrong swapping them out for peanuts every now and then.

1 pound carrots, shredded (3 cups)

Zest of 1 lime

Juice of 1 lime (1 tablespoon)

1 tablespoon toasted sesame oil

2 teaspoons soy sauce

3 scallions sliced, green part only

2 tablespoons chopped fresh cilantro

⅓ cup toasted sliced almonds

8 ounces lo mein noodles

1. Stir together the carrots, lime zest, lime juice, sesame oil, and soy sauce in a medium bowl. Add the scallions and cilantro. Reserve 1 tablespoon of the almonds. Stir the remaining almonds into the carrots. Refrigerate while you make the noodles.

2. Cook the lo mein noodles according to the package directions, removing them from the heat while they are still slightly al dente. Rinse with cold water as they sit in a colander in the sink and drain. This will cool the noodles and stop the cooking.

3. Transfer the noodles to a serving bowl. Spoon the carrots over the noodles and garnish with the reserved almonds before serving.

THEOPOLIS VINEYARDS

THEODORA LEE, YORKVILLE

Owner and vintner is only a sampling of the roles Theodora Lee manages from day to day. When she's not tending to the 5 acres of Petite Sirah she planted in the Yorkville Highlands of the Anderson Valley and making wine, she's managing her law practice as a trial attorney in San Francisco.

Theodora carries an infectious energy that allows her to incorporate all the things important to her into her daily life, including family, law, community, and wine, in that order. You can't help but feel empowered by this energy when you spend time with her.

She was initially attracted to the Yorkville Highlands of Anderson Valley because it was affordable and had established itself as a source of consistently noteworthy wines. She explains that as the afternoon air turns hot, cool breezes cross the region from the nearby Pacific Ocean and frigid nighttime temperatures preserve the grape's acidity. "Mature tannins in the red wines are the result; they are long and complex without being overpowering. Yorkville Highlands' fruit ripens evenly, with acidity, structure, and richness balancing each other," says Theodora.

While being a winemaker is a creative outlet for her, using this role to foster positive change in her community is a priority. This is why she established the Theopolis Vineyards Diversity Fund for the Department of Viticulture and Enology at the University of California, Davis. The fund provides one scholarship each year to students interested in viticulture and enology, or research and vineyard management related to those career paths. "Preference is given to students who are underrepresented or understand barriers to entering the industry. I established this fund to encourage future vintners, especially women of color. As one of the few African American women who owns her own vineyard, I hope to inspire others to become vintners," says Theodora.

Theodora enjoys her work as a lawyer and a winemaker. So much so that she doesn't consider it work. "I love being able to help my clients resolve complex legal issues. I also absolutely love providing pleasure in the bottle for my wine family. So, I am not really working, but living life, to its fullest," she says.

Vegetable Lasagna

SERVES 8

I can't remember ordering vegetable lasagna at a restaurant, and it's because I grew up with a version that was so good, I knew I'd never find another to compete with it. On special occasions, my mom would make her vegetable lasagna—noodles layered with a white sauce, spinach, and broccoli, sometimes carrots. I've included a few more farm-fresh ingredients in this version, such as both carrots and zucchini instead of one or the other, and added fresh herbs, but the flavors are true to the original version of my childhood.

2 tablespoons extra-virgin olive oil

2 cups finely chopped broccoli
    (about 8 ounces florets)

1½ cups shredded carrots (about 8 ounces)

1½ cups shredded zucchini (about 1 medium)

2 cups fresh spinach

1 tablespoon minced fresh basil

1 tablespoon minced fresh oregano

1 teaspoon fine sea salt

One 15- or 16-ounce container whole-milk ricotta

2 large eggs

½ teaspoon ground black pepper

3 tablespoons unsalted butter, plus
    more for baking pan

¼ cup all-purpose flour

2½ cups whole milk

½ cup freshly grated Parmesan (about 1½ ounces)

12 lasagna noodles, cooked according
    to package directions

8 ounces whole-milk mozzarella,
    shredded (about 2 cups)

Small basil and oregano leaves for garnish

1. Heat the olive oil in a large skillet over medium-high. Add the broccoli, carrots, and zucchini. Cook until the vegetables are tender with just a bit of bite left to them, 5 to 7 minutes. Add the spinach, basil, oregano, and ½ teaspoon of the salt. Cook until the spinach wilts, 1 to 2 more minutes. Remove from the heat and set aside.

2. Stir together the ricotta, eggs, and pepper in a small bowl until combined, then set aside.

3. Melt the butter in a medium saucepan over medium-high heat. Lower the heat to medium and sprinkle in the flour, whisking vigorously as you do so until a paste forms. This happens very quickly, usually less than a minute.

4. Lower the heat further to medium-low and slowly add the milk as you continue to whisk. Whisk until all the flour paste is incorporated into the milk and the liquid is smooth.

5. Increase the heat back to medium and whisk often as the sauce begins to bubble and thicken. Once it reaches the consistency to coat the back of a spoon, about 4 minutes, remove it from the heat and stir in the remaining ½ teaspoon of salt and the Parmesan. Stir until smooth.

6. Preheat the oven to 350°F.

7. Butter a 9-by-13-inch baking pan. Spread 2 tablespoons of the white sauce thinly along the bottom of the pan. Reserve ½ cup of the remaining sauce and set aside.

8. Arrange four lasagna noodles in the bottom of the pan. Top with half of the ricotta mixture and spread over the noodles. Next, layer with half of the vegetables. Top with half of the remaining white sauce and spread it over the vegetables.

9. Repeat with another layer of four noodles, the remaining ricotta, the rest of the vegetables, and the other half of the sauce.

10. Top with the remaining four noodles. Thinly spread the reserved ½ cup of sauce over the noodles. Top evenly with the mozzarella.

11. Cover with foil and bake for 40 minutes. Remove the foil and bake for 10 more minutes, or until the edges of the lasagna are golden brown. Let rest for at least 5 minutes before slicing to serve.

Rice and Kale Salad with Herb Vinaigrette and Parmesan

SERVES 4 TO 6

This is a hearty salad that will carry you through autumn and winter, when an abundance of produce is in shorter supply. Either brown rice or a wild rice blend is a good match for the pleasantly bitter kale. Both curly kale and lacinato kale work well in this recipe, but don't be afraid to get creative with some purple kale as well. The salad has deep savory flavors as it is, but sometimes I'll toss in some diced dried apricots or dried sweet cherries to mix things up.

1 bunch kale, thinly sliced (6 cups)

1 tablespoon extra-virgin olive oil

¼ teaspoon fine sea salt

½ shallot, thinly sliced (¼ cup)

½ teaspoon grated lemon zest

1 cup uncooked brown or wild rice blend,
   cooked according to package directions

Shaved Parmesan for serving

Herb Vinaigrette

3 tablespoons extra-virgin olive oil

2 tablespoons grated Parmesan

Juice of ½ lemon (1 tablespoon)

½ teaspoon chopped fresh basil

½ teaspoon fine sea salt

¼ teaspoon ground black pepper

¼ teaspoon minced fresh rosemary

¼ teaspoon minced fresh thyme

1. Place the kale in a large bowl and drizzle with the olive oil. Add the salt and use clean or gloved hands to massage the oil into the kale until it turns dark green and wilts slightly, 1 minute.

2. Stir in the shallot, lemon zest, and rice.

3. Make the dressing: Combine all the dressing ingredients in a small jar with a lid. Shake well until they are mixed. Alternatively, you can whisk together the ingredients in a small bowl.

4. Pour the dressing over the salad and stir well. Serve right away or refrigerate for up to 24 hours before serving. Top with shaved Parmesan just before eating.

KODA FARMS

ROBIN KODA, SOUTH DOS PALOS

"My mission, my goal, is to educate people that rice is not just a bland filler carb," says Robin Koda. She owns and operates Koda Farms with her brother Ross, a farm that grows, harvests, mills, and packages Japanese-style rice and flours. The farm is a family legacy that began with their grandfather who first started farming in California in the late 1910s.

"When people think of rice as a carrier for soy sauce, butter, or gravy, then they are not appreciating rice for itself. They are eating the condiments they are putting on it," says Robin. "I explain to people that there are really great varieties of rice that should stand up on their own." Much of her work is educating consumers on what a revelation eating high-quality rice can be, and customers return to tell her just that.

While the rice they grow is Japanese style and an ideal choice for sushi and mochi, its versatility reaches far beyond Japanese cuisine. "Harold McGee and Alton Brown were the first two purveyors of science of food to me. Harold McGee was once talking about how risotto strains of rice are largely based on Japonica," says Robin. That was like a lightbulb going on for her and has led to her sharing how versatile their rice is in cooking across cultures. Customers and culinary professionals have been longtime advocates for using their rice in such dishes as risotto and paella.

Their organic Kokuho Rose Heirloom Rice is available as a premium medium-grain white rice and as a whole-grain brown rice. "The white rice is softer and more fragrant, while the brown rice is more robust," says Robin.

It's their sweet short-grain rice, though, that gets a lot of the attention. Sho-Chiku-Bai sweet rice is a glutinous, or sticky, rice that is used for Japanese mochi as well as Chinese dim sum and Filipino *bibingka*. Koda Farms was the first commercial grower of sweet rice in California, and remains the number one seller of sweet rice in the United States. They brought this rice, and the flour made from it, to the American market back in the 1940s, and we still get to enjoy it today.

Ginger Lemongrass California Rice Bowls

SERVES 6

The California roll may not have been invented in this state, but I'd argue that we have the best ingredients for making it. Between the terroir-driven rice grown throughout our Central Valley, to fresh avocados and sweet Dungeness crab, there is nothing like a California roll from California. This recipe is a twist on that traditional sushi roll with avocado, crab, and cucumber, served in a bowl. Each component gets a flavor upgrade, starting with rice that is flooded with bright lemongrass, spicy ginger, and savory garlic. In this recipe, I like to use a medium-grain white rice, such as the heirloom Kokuho Rose from Koda Farms (page 43).

Tamari-Marinated Cucumbers

¼ cup tamari

¼ cup seasoned rice vinegar

2 teaspoons sugar

2 teaspoons black sesame seeds

6 Persian cucumbers (about 1 pound), thinly sliced

Rice Bowls

1 tablespoon extra-virgin olive oil

2 garlic cloves, minced

1 tablespoon minced fresh ginger

1 tablespoon minced fresh lemongrass

2 cups uncooked medium-grain white rice, rinsed

4 cups water

1 teaspoon fine sea salt, plus more to taste

1½ pounds cooked Dungeness crabmeat

3 avocados

Black sesame seeds or furikake for garnish

Note: The cucumbers will have plenty of flavor after resting for one hour, but I like to make them the morning that I plan to make these bowls for dinner, so that the flavors have plenty of time to infuse the crunchy pieces. I use small Persian or cocktail cucumbers, but an English cucumber can be substituted.

1. Make the cucumbers: Stir together the tamari, rice vinegar, sugar, and black sesame seeds in a medium bowl with a lid. Stir in the cucumbers, ensuring each piece is in contact with the marinade. Cover and refrigerate for at least 1 hour.

2. Make the rice bowls: Heat the olive oil in a large pot over medium-high. Add the garlic, ginger, and lemongrass and stir for 1 minute until all ingredients glisten with oil and you can smell their aroma. Add the rice and cook for 2 minutes, stirring often, until coated in oil and it begins to smell lightly nutty.

3. Lower the heat to medium and stir in the water. Bring to a simmer and cook, partially covered, for 10 minutes, until al dente. Adjust the heat as needed to maintain a gentle simmer. There will still be starchy water present around the rice.

4. Place the lid on the pot and remove it from the heat. Let stand for 5 minutes.

5. Stir the teaspoon of salt into the rice, replace the lid, and let sit 5 more minutes. Fluff the rice with a fork. All the water should be absorbed and the rice tender.

6. To assemble the bowls, place a generous cup of rice in each of six bowls. Top each with 4 ounces of crabmeat and a spoonful of cucumbers with their marinade.

7. Once all are assembled, halve each avocado and remove the pit and peel. Slice the halves and add a sliced avocado half to each bowl. Sprinkle with black sesame seeds or furikake, and season with additional salt, if desired.

Smoky Tomato, Kale, and Mushroom Marinara

MAKES ABOUT 3 CUPS

This recipe is my favorite way to switch up basic marinara during summer, when tomatoes are plentiful. While some tomato varieties are best suited for sauce, this recipe doesn't judge based on variety. The tomatoes are grilled in packets, creating a tender, juicy combination with a hint of smokiness that blends well regardless of whether you have extra Roma, beefsteak, or a rare, colorful heirloom variety. Because the sauce is made on the grill and in a skillet on the stove, I often grill the tomatoes whenever we're cooking outside and store them in the refrigerator until I'm ready to make the marinara the next day. Serve it over hot pasta or bake it into a cheesy pasta casserole.

Grilled Tomatoes

2 pounds tomatoes, chopped

1 tablespoon extra-virgin olive oil

6 garlic cloves, peeled

¾ teaspoon fine sea salt

Marinara

2 tablespoons extra-virgin olive oil

1½ teaspoons balsamic vinegar

1½ teaspoons sugar

8 ounces cremini mushrooms, finely chopped

5 kale leaves, stemmed and finely chopped

1 teaspoon fine sea salt, or to taste

1 teaspoon dried basil

1 teaspoon dried oregano

½ teaspoon smoked paprika

½ teaspoon crushed red pepper flakes, or to taste

¼ teaspoon ground black pepper

Notes: Chop the mushrooms finely. Once they make it into the sauce, they nearly have the consistency of ground beef, giving it a meaty texture. You can pulse them in a food processor instead of chopping them by hand; just be sure to avoid turning them into a mushroom paste. Any variety of kale will work in the sauce. I often use curly leaf, but lacinato adds nice flavor and texture, too.

1. Make the tomatoes: Preheat a grill to medium, 375° to 400°F. Tear off three 14-inch pieces of heavy-duty aluminum foil.

2. Divide the tomatoes among the three sheets of foil, making a pile in the center of each sheet. Use 1 tablespoon of the olive oil to drizzle over all three of the tomato piles.Top each pile with two garlic cloves and ¼ teaspoon of the salt. Turn the sheets of foil so that a short side faces you. Fold in the right and left sides over the tomatoes, then bring the top and bottom sides together over the tomatoes and roll them down, creating a sealed packet.

3. Place the packets on the grill and cook for 20 to 25 minutes, until the tomatoes and garlic are tender. Let sit until cool enough to handle.

4. Make the marinara: Open the tomato packets. Transfer the tomatoes with the garlic and juices to a blender. Add 1 tablespoon of the olive oil, the balsamic vinegar, and the sugar to the blender. Puree on high speed until the tomato sauce is completely smooth. Set aside.

5. Heat a skillet over medium-high and add the mushrooms. Let the mushrooms cook to release their moisture, stirring occasionally. After 1 to 2 minutes, liquid will begin to bubble around them. Continue to cook until all the liquid has been absorbed back into the mushrooms and is no longer in the pan, about 1 more minute.

6. Add the remaining 1 tablespoon of olive oil and the kale and cook, stirring often, until the kale is tender, about 3 more minutes. Stir in the salt, basil, oregano, smoked paprika, red pepper flakes, and black pepper.

7. Lower the heat to medium-low and stir in the tomato sauce. Simmer until thickened, about 5 minutes. Add more salt or other seasonings to taste, if desired. Serve warm or store in the refrigerator for up to 3 days.

BLT Salad Stuffed Tomatoes with Garlic Dill Dressing

SERVES 6

This twist on the classic sandwich highlights heirloom tomato season, which is my favorite thing about summer. It's a recipe I first made years ago using small tomatoes from my garden. Once I discovered big, colorful heirloom tomatoes, this plated recipe became the star of the table. You can use any type of tomato, but an assortment of colors creates a fun spread of options for guests to choose from. Depending on the size of your tomatoes and how much of the center you scoop out, you may have some extra salad. I like to serve it alongside the tomatoes so that everyone can add it to their plates.

Garlic Dill Dressing

2 tablespoons plain Greek yogurt

2 tablespoons mayonnaise

3 tablespoons whole milk

1 garlic clove, grated

1 tablespoon minced fresh chives

1 tablespoon minced fresh dill

¼ teaspoon fine sea salt

⅛ teaspoon ground black pepper

BLT Salad

1 tablespoon salted butter

3 tablespoons panko bread crumbs

6 medium-to-large assorted heirloom tomatoes

1 head green leaf lettuce, finely chopped (about 6 cups)

1 ounce freshly grated Parmesan (⅓ cup)

5 fresh basil leaves, minced

8 slices bacon, cooked and crumbled

1. Make the dressing: Stir together the yogurt and mayonnaise in a small bowl. Stir in the milk until smooth. Add the garlic, chives, dill, salt, and pepper and stir well until all the ingredients are combined. Place in the refrigerator until ready to serve.

2. Make the salad: Heat the butter in a small skillet over medium-high. Add the bread crumbs and cook, stirring often, until lightly toasted and crunchy, 1 to 2 minutes. Set aside.

3. Core each of the tomatoes, removing the center of the fruit but leaving the tomato intact to create a small bowl to hold the salad. Arrange the tomatoes on a serving platter or put each on its own serving plate.

4. Combine the lettuce, Parmesan, and basil in a large bowl. Toss well.

5. Finely chop 2 tablespoons of the bacon crumbles until they resemble crumbs. Set aside.

6. Add the remaining bacon to the salad, along with the dressing. Toss well to mix all the ingredients and evenly distribute the dressing and bacon throughout the salad.

7. Fill each cored tomato with salad and pile it up high on top. Sprinkle each with the panko bread crumbs and reserved bacon crumbs. Serve right away with any extra salad on the side.

Stuffed Indian Eggplant with Goat Cheese and Prosciutto

SERVES 6

Indian eggplants are often labeled "baby eggplant" at farmers' markets. While a dark, purple-black skin is common, you can also find hybrid varieties that are speckled purple and white and light purple. Their tender skin and small size are what makes them so good for stuffing with local goat cheese, walnuts, and honey. Once wrapped in prosciutto and grilled, they turn into an earthy sweet and savory two-to-three bite starter for an outdoor meal. I try to choose eggplants that are about 2½ inches in length so there is room to scoop out the seeds and stuff in the cheese. The fresher the eggplant, the better. You want a tender, edible skin to enjoy. Keep the stem intact to hold in the stuffing, but discard it when eating your stuffed eggplant.

12 Indian eggplants (about 1½ pounds)

Extra-virgin olive oil

4 ounces chèvre, at room temperature

⅓ cup raw walnut pieces, finely chopped

1 tablespoon minced fresh chives

1 teaspoon honey

12 slices prosciutto (about 8 ounces)

1. Heat the grill to medium, 350°F. Rub each eggplant lightly with olive oil.

2. Grill each eggplant for 7 to 8 minutes, flipping once or twice while they cook. The skin should darken, and they should give a little when squeezed gently with tongs, indicating that the inside is just starting to become tender. Remove them from the grill and let sit until cool enough to handle.

3. While the eggplants cool, stir together the chèvre, walnuts, chives, and honey in a small bowl.

4. Slit each eggplant down one side, but don't cut all the way through. Use a spoon to carefully scoop out a small spoonful of seeds. You aren't cleaning out the whole eggplant or all the flesh, just enough to create space for a little filling.

5. Spoon about 1 tablespoon of filling into the eggplant and press the cut sides back together around the filling. Some can take a little more, some less, depending on the exact size of each eggplant.

6. Wrap each eggplant with a slice of prosciutto, being sure to completely cover the slit and wrap it around the sides and bottom so that all the eggplant is covered except the stem.

7. Grill the eggplants for 3 to 5 more minutes, flipping once, until the prosciutto crisps on the outside and the eggplants are warmed through. Serve right away.

DRESSER WINERY

CATHERINE AND KORY BURKE, PASO ROBLES

I'm drawn to people who jump in and take the kind of chances that can change the course of their lives. After all, that's how I ended up in California in the first place. It turns out that food and beverage are where all of us with these characteristics tend to congregate. It's what led me to Catherine and Kory Burke of Dresser Winery.

With no background in the wine industry, they made the decision to move to Paso Robles on day two of their first visit to the area. Three months later, and a few days before the birth of their daughter Kaia, they found a small property. Less than two years after Kory began apprenticing with a local winemaker, they were given the opportunity to buy his small, commercial vineyard and winery. They both quit their day jobs and went all in.

Kory's goal from the start has been to make wine less pretentious and more approachable. "It's why the casual tastings he does are so inviting," says Catherine. This approachable nature is what makes Catherine and Kory's winery a place where you can enjoy some of the best the Paso Robles region has to offer while learning more about wine, whether you consider yourself a novice or an expert. It's an experience with all the joy and none of the judgment.

The boutique, family-owned winery, with a striking black barn, sits at the bottom of the vineyard lined with vines of Zinfandel, Syrah, Petite Sirah, and Cabernet Sauvignon. One of their top wines is the SFR, or the S**t-Faced Red. "The name harkens back to what can happen when we're not careful with how much we taste when we are creating our blends during our blending trials," Kory says with a laugh. The wine is a blend of all the varietals above but it's always Petite Sirah dominant. "Pair this one with a rough week at work or let it stand up to meatier pairings. Maybe grab your favorite person and enjoy it on its own on a cool fall evening or cold winter night by the fireplace," says Kory.

Grilled Eggplant and Lentil Spread

MAKES ABOUT 2 CUPS

This smooth legume-based spread is best described as baba ghanoush meets hummus. It's my snack of choice during summer, when eggplants are in season. Grilling the eggplant adds a hint of smokiness and the lentils become almost whipped, creating a light, airy spread with a rich earthy heartiness. It can serve as dip for pita bread or vegetables, but don't pass up spooning it inside a grilled vegetable sandwich or using it as a substitute for refried beans in vegetarian tacos.

1 cup dried green lentils, rinsed

3 cups water

3 garlic cloves, peeled

1½ teaspoons fine sea salt

3 Japanese eggplants

6 tablespoons extra-virgin olive oil

2 tablespoons tahini

1 tablespoon chopped fresh parsley

1 teaspoon fresh lemon juice

¼ teaspoon ground black pepper

Extra-virgin olive oil, plus more
    for grilling and serving

Flake smoked sea salt for serving

Fresh parsley for garnish

Grilled pita bread strips for serving

1. Combine the lentils, water, and garlic cloves in a medium saucepan with a lid. Stir in ½ teaspoon of the salt. Bring to a boil over medium-high heat. Lower the heat so that the lentils maintain a simmer and partially cover with a lid. Cook, stirring often to mash the lentils and garlic, until the lentils are completely softened to the point that you can mash them, and all the water has been absorbed, about 20 minutes. Remove from the heat and let the lentils cool.

2. Preheat a grill to medium, 375° to 400°F. Rub each eggplant lightly with olive oil and prick each in a few places with a fork. Grill for 10 minutes, flipping once, until the skin turns brown, the eggplant shrivels, and the interior is completely softened. Remove from the grill, slit each eggplant open with a knife, and let them sit until cool enough to handle.

3. Transfer the lentils to a blender. Add 2 tablespoons of the olive oil, the tahini, chopped parsley, lemon juice, remaining teaspoon of salt, and the pepper. Scrape the inside of the eggplants, removing as much of the flesh as possible; discard the charred skin and stems. Transfer the eggplant flesh to the blender.

4. Pulse to begin blending the ingredients. The blender contents will be thick and you may need to scrape the sides to continue.

5. Once the eggplant is blended into the lentils, add the remaining 4 tablespoons of olive oil. Puree on high speed for 30 seconds, or until the spread is smooth with a creamy, whipped consistency.

6. Transfer to a serving bowl or plate, drizzle with more olive oil, sprinkle with smoked sea salt, and top with parsley. Serve with grilled pita bread for dipping.

Summer Squash Soup

MAKES 2 QUARTS

I've lived in hot places where I steered clear of turning on the oven during summer. This recipe is a celebration of my love for living in cooler climates. Here on California's Central Coast, our foggy summer days pair well with a roasted summer vegetable soup like this one. I use a mix of summer squashes, such as zucchini and yellow crookneck. This soup is light, creamy, and fragrant with rosemary. It's also best paired with a hunk of your favorite bread.

6 assorted summer squash (about 3 pounds)

1 russet potato, peeled and diced

1 tablespoon fresh rosemary leaves

2 tablespoons extra-virgin olive oil

1¼ teaspoons fine sea salt, or to taste

4 cups chicken stock

¼ teaspoon ground black pepper, or to taste

Chopped fresh rosemary for garnish

1. Preheat the oven to 400°F. Line a baking sheet with parchment paper.

2. Trim away the ends of the squash and cut them into large slices. Place the pieces on the prepared baking sheet, along with the diced potato. It will be a tight fit. If it doesn't all fit on one baking sheet, feel free to use a second and rotate them in the oven while roasting.

3. Sprinkle the rosemary leaves over the vegetables. Drizzle with the olive oil and add ¼ teaspoon of the salt. Move the vegetables around to coat them in the oil.

4. Roast for 20 minutes, until the squash dries at the edges and becomes tender. Carefully stir the vegetables and roast for 10 more minutes, until the squash and potatoes are completely tender. Remove from the oven and let sit until cool enough to work with, about 30 minutes.

5. Transfer the vegetables to a large blender. It will be full. If it's too full for your blender, work in batches. Puree until the vegetables are smooth. You will likely need to use the wand to stir as it purees. If it is too thick, add a little of the chicken stock.

6. Heat the chicken stock in a medium soup pot over medium-high for about 5 minutes. Slowly stir in the contents of the blender. Lower the heat to medium and stir in the remaining teaspoon of salt and the pepper. Add more of each to your taste, if desired. Warm for about 5 minutes, until heated through.

7. Serve garnished with rosemary.

BROWN GIRL FARMS

ASHLEE AND JEN JOHNSON-GEISSE, HAYWARD

"As a Black farmer, I often say that farming is an ancestral legacy that we hold inside of us. That legacy is waiting to be cultivated if we desire to do so," says Ashlee Johnson-Geisse. Ashlee accessed her ancestral legacy of farming when creating Brown Girl Farms in 2020. The farm began as a patio garden and now she and her wife, Jen, have an urban farm in the East Bay city of Hayward.

Among the many African American Heritage crops they grow, Ashlee's favorite is purple tree collards, a beautiful variety of collard green. "Being a Queer Black farmer, it's important to me that the foods that matter to us within the Black community as well as the stories and memories of our connection to these foods be cultivated and grown by Black farmers," says Ashlee.

Their farm also incorporates African Indigenous Agroecology, a method of agriculture that blends Indigenous knowledge with science and the natural ecosystem. They produce food on less than an acre and their property is sloped. Incorporating permanent terraced beds, a practice used in East Africa, helps them maximize their space. Intercropping, cultivating two or more crops on the same field, allows them to grow more in a small space and attracts beneficial insects to the farm.

The chickens they keep provide eggs, but they also represent an important part of African American culture. "Enslaved peoples were sometimes allowed to keep chickens on plantations and would sell or trade meat and eggs. In villages across the African diaspora, chickens and other birds like guinea fowl have been raised as well," Ashlee says.

Ashlee and Jen are advocates for both the Black farming community and the Queer farming community. "It is important to me to be able to build up a network and support and hire others who hold some of the same intersecting identities," says Ashlee.

Through Brown Girl Farms, she and Jen are ensuring the African American food heritage of the past is not lost while they simultaneously work toward a future for farming that provides a diverse, supported, and welcoming space for everyone who has a passion for growing food.

Caramelized Onion Dip

MAKES 1½ CUPS

I've worked with the National Onion Association for several years, and many of its growers are right here in California. Defining truly caramelized onions has always been a topic of our discussions when creating recipes. Caramelizing onions goes beyond browning them. Their color darkens so deeply, and the flavors intensify so sweetly that when complete, they melt in your mouth like an onion jam. It's a task that takes at least 45 minutes of your time, but in the end, you'll have no regrets for investing it. This recipe takes those onions and purees them into a creamy dip that can be served with chopped veggies and potato chips or spread on crackers.

2 tablespoons extra-virgin olive oil

3 medium yellow onions, chopped

1 cup sour cream

4 ounces cream cheese, softened

2 tablespoons chopped fresh chives,
    plus more for garnish

1 teaspoon fine sea salt

¼ teaspoon ground black pepper

Notes: A medium onion is roughly 2½ to 3 inches in diameter. I use a cast-iron pan for caramelizing onions, but other types of skillets work well, too.

1. Heat the olive oil in a large skillet over medium-high. Add the onions and cook until they are glistening with oil and begin to soften, about 3 minutes. Lower the heat to medium-low. Continue to stir occasionally as they cook. Adjust the heat as needed to ensure they don't darken too quickly. You want them to cook slowly and evenly.

2. Once they reach about 20 minutes of cooking time, begin watching them more closely. They will need to be stirred more often and the heat turned to low. Continue to cook for 25 to 35 more minutes, until the onions are caramel brown in color and completely soft and mashable. Remove from the heat and let cool to room temperature.

3. Combine the sour cream, cream cheese, chives, salt, and pepper in a blender or food processor. Reserve a couple of teaspoons of caramelized onions to garnish the dip. Add the remaining caramelized onions to the blender.

4. Begin blending on low speed to mix the ingredients, then increase the speed to medium-high. Puree until smooth, about 20 seconds. You will likely need to scrape down the sides of the container during blending, to ensure all the onions and chives are pureed.

5. Chill for 30 minutes before garnishing with the reserved onions and chives to serve.

Roasted Purple Cauliflower with Smoked Almond Garlic Crumble

SERVES 6

Cauliflower was doomed the day we all decided to make it a health food substitute for potatoes and pizza crust. It was inevitable that we'd get tired of it and swear it off our menus forever. It's a shame because, as a side dish, it pairs well with so many meats or it can stand all on its own as a vegan option. I think we should all celebrate cauliflower for the vegetable it was meant to be. And what better for a celebration than choosing one of the many colors of cauliflower that can be found all over farmers' markets. When Tanaka Farms (page 34) gave me a stunning head of purple cauliflower during my visit, I knew I had to pair it with one of my savory crumbles. Garlic and smoked almonds load this roasted cauliflower with flavor and deliver a crunch that complements the tender vegetable.

Cauliflower

1 large head purple cauliflower, cut in about 2-inch florets

2 tablespoons extra-virgin olive oil

¼ teaspoon fine sea salt

¼ teaspoon ground black pepper

Almond Garlic Crumble

2 tablespoons extra-virgin olive oil

1 cup smoked almonds, chopped

3 garlic cloves, minced

2 tablespoons chopped fresh chives

3 tablespoons panko bread crumbs

Notes: This recipe gives you a lot of nutty crumble. I like to layer it in with the vegetables for serving and have extra on the table. If you want to use less, just store it in an airtight container for up to 24 hours and top tomorrow's vegetables with it. It also works well on asparagus and broccoli. Most smoked almonds are also salted, but feel free to salt the final dish to taste when serving if you prefer more.

1. Preheat the oven to 400°F.

2. Make the cauliflower: Spread the florets on a baking sheet. Drizzle with the oil and sprinkle with the salt and pepper. Stir the cauliflower so that it is well coated, then spread it into a single layer.

3. Bake for 10 minutes, or until it just begins to soften. Remove from the oven and stir. Bake for 10 to 15 more minutes, until it is tender and begins to brown.

4. While the cauliflower bakes, make the crumble: Heat the olive oil in a large skillet over medium-high. Add the almonds and cook, stirring, until aromatic, 1 minute. Add the garlic and continue to stir to lightly cook it, 2 minutes. Stir in the chives and the bread crumbs and cook for 30 seconds to combine all the ingredients. Remove from the heat.

5. When the cauliflower is roasted, transfer half of it to a platter. Top with a third of the crumble, add the rest of the cauliflower, then another third of the crumble. Serve the remaining crumble on the side.

ADMIRAL MALTINGS

RON SILBERSTEIN, ALAMEDA

The first brewery I went to in California, long before I moved to this state, was ThirstyBear Brewing Company in San Francisco. It was the first and only organic brewery in the city when it opened in 1996 and it was owned by Ron Silberstein. Unfortunately, the brewery closed in 2021 as California's longest-operating brew pub in San Francisco, but the values held by Ron live on through his current work helping California brewers, distillers, and even bakers to make their products with local ingredients.

"I had always had a connection to ingredients," says Ron. This interest in ingredients and the impact of how they are grown is what led him to create Admiral Maltings with fellow brewery owner Dave McLean, and organic farmer and small-batch malter Curtis Davenport.

As recently as 2015, not a single brewery in California was using barley that was grown and then malted in the state. Yet California has a long history of growing malting-quality barley that's well adapted to our environment. With the increase in consumer interest to buy local products and know where their food and drink come from, Ron saw a need that Admiral Maltings could fulfill.

"We source from those who grow in California and who grow a barley variety that was developed here," says Ron. They work with farmers who use sustainable methods, such as no-till agriculture and usage of cover crops, and who utilize animal grazing to maximize soil health.

Grains must be malted for use in brewing and distilling. Admiral Maltings uses an ancient, artisan method called floor malting and provides freshly kilned grains to their customers. While, in general, malt involves a simple process, Ron

explains the complexities of malting grain by comparing it to wine making. "A vintner can take a grape and smash it and they have fermentable sugars. Yeast can immediately ferment the sugars of that grape, but they cannot ferment the really long chain of starches in a barley seed," he says. The matter around the starches in a grain must be broken down to become accessible. "If you smash a barley seed and you add water and yeast, you'll get at the most bread, but you will not get any fermentable sugars. You could never get beer," he says.

Soaking the barley tricks it into thinking it's going to grow so that it just barely germinates. The drying stops the sprouting and holds all the now accessible sugars in place. "We take the grain, put it in a tank, and soak it. We spread it on the floor and sprout it and then we put it in a giant convection oven, called a kiln, where we dry it and give it color and flavor," says Ron. The malted grain becomes a packet of water-soluble sugars and enzymes ready to be used by brewers or distillers throughout the state, creating a bridge that connects our farmers to what's in our glass.

Green Grape, Arugula, and Spelt Salad

SERVES 4

From midsummer through fall, table grapes ranging from light green to deep purple are piled on tables throughout the farmers' markets of California. It's that time of year that I like to pull together a simple grain salad like this one. I use spelt here, but any chewy, cooked grain from wheat berries to farro or Kamut can be substituted.

½ cup spelt berries, rinsed

1 cup vegetable stock

½ cup water

1½ cups green grapes, halved

¼ large red onion, thinly sliced

⅓ cup toasted slivered almonds

2 tablespoons extra-virgin olive oil

1 tablespoon Champagne vinegar

½ teaspoon minced shallot

¼ teaspoon fine sea salt

⅛ teaspoon ground black pepper

1 cup packed arugula

1. Stir together the spelt berries, stock, and water in a medium saucepan. Bring to a boil, then partially cover and lower the heat to a simmer. Cook until the grains are tender but still chewy and the liquid is absorbed, 22 to 25 minutes.

2. While the spelt cooks, combine the grapes, onion, and almonds in a medium bowl.

3. Combine the olive oil, vinegar, shallot, salt, and pepper in a small mason jar. Cover with the lid and shake until the ingredients are blended. Alternatively, you can whisk the dressing in a small bowl.

4. Drain the cooked grains and rinse well with cold water. Add the grains to the bowl that contains the grapes. Pour in the dressing and stir well. Just before serving, stir in the arugula. Serve at room temperature or slightly chilled.

Roasted Winter Squash with Onions and Blue Cheese

SERVES 4 TO 6

Traveling gave me my first true introduction to the versatility of winter squash. Long before we became pumpkin crazy in the United States with coffees, cakes, and pies, winter squash was used in other culinary cultures as a savory ingredient. This combination is one I discovered while living in Brazil, but it fits nicely in California, where late summer brings green fields dotted with orange pumpkins and markets fill up with beautiful heirloom varieties. Soils in the state also grow acres of onions, and our pastures produce some of the best blue cheese available. I like to use Point Reyes (page 151). Original Blue with the recipe along with butternut squash or a kabocha.

2¼ pounds winter squash, peeled and
    cut in 1-inch cubes (6 cups)

½ small yellow onion, sliced

1 tablespoon extra-virgin olive oil

½ teaspoon fine sea salt

¼ teaspoon minced fresh rosemary

¼ teaspoon ground black pepper

2 ounces blue cheese, crumbled

1. Preheat the oven to 400°F. Line a baking sheet with parchment paper.

2. Spread the squash and the onion on the prepared baking sheet. Drizzle with the olive oil and sprinkle with ¼ teaspoon of the salt and the rosemary. Stir to coat all the pieces and then spread into a single layer.

3. Bake for 10 minutes. Carefully stir the squash, making an effort to turn over all the pieces. Bake for an additional 10 to 15 minutes, until the squash is fork-tender.

4. Remove from the oven. Sprinkle with the remaining ¼ teaspoon of salt and the pepper. Transfer to a serving dish, top with the blue cheese, and serve warm.

COASTAL ROOTS FARM

ENCINITAS

"Regenerative agriculture, and feeding people, is really what we are here for," says Jess Arroyo. She's the marketing and events manager at Coastal Roots Farm, a nonprofit Jewish community farm, a regenerative organic farm that pulls from ancient Jewish values in its agricultural practices and in educational programming. Along with feeding the community, Coastal Roots teaches environmental and social justice through those values to the students who visit the farm.

As a regenerative farm, it grows food with a focus on seasonality and soil health. "For everything we take, we are putting more into the soil," says Jess. The process is planting the food, growing it, harvesting it, and then moving in the chickens in their mobile coops. The chickens help with pest management, but they also fertilize the soil. These practices help them grow the large variety of organic produce, such as root vegetables, leafy greens, and melons, that the farm provides to the community.

"Equitable food access is huge for us," says Jess. Over 70 percent of the 80,000 pounds of food Coastal Roots grows in a year is donated to

the community. This happens through both its distribution efforts and its on-site farm stand.

The farm stand operates as pay-what-you-can food store. Anyone from the community can come and get free produce. Once they reach a $30 value for their free food, the stand operates as an anonymous pay system and suggested donation. People simply pay what they can for that day. "Our farm stand, for a lot of people, is the only place they are getting fresh, organic food," Jess says.

Through donors, corporate partnerships, fundraising events, and grants, Coastal Roots can provide fresh food to the community along with educational information, such as recipe cards. The farm works with older adult communities, Holocaust survivors and their families, military families, and Tribal communities. Sometimes, it simply provides food, but also assists with garden build projects.

"I love being part of an organization that is feeding so many people, and nourishing so many people, but also that is teaching and creating young climate activists here who will then fight for our planet," says Jess.

Coastal Roots' Mediterranean Stuffed Collard Greens

SERVES 4 TO 6

I'd never thought of making a wrap out of a green like collards until Coastal Roots Farm introduced me to this recipe. The creation of team member Julia Meyer, the recipe folds a filling of nutrient-rich quinoa, lentils, aromatic spices, and fresh herbs inside tender leaves of collard greens. The baked wraps are a treat for the taste buds on their own, but Julia says, "They can also be covered with tomato sauce before being baked. Enjoy with toasted bread, salad, or just about anything!"

1 bunch collard greens (10 to 12 leaves)

1 tablespoon extra-virgin olive oil

1 large yellow onion, diced

2 medium carrots, diced

1 teaspoon fine sea salt, or to taste

½ teaspoon ground black pepper, or to taste

¼ teaspoon ground cardamom

¼ teaspoon ground cinnamon

¼ teaspoon ground cumin

2½ cups cooked brown or green lentils

2½ cups cooked quinoa

1 cup golden raisins

Zest of 1 lemon

Juice of 1 lemon (2 tablespoons)

¼ cup chopped fresh dill

¼ cup chopped fresh mint

¼ cup chopped fresh parsley

Olive oil for baking

Lemon slices for baking

Notes: The filling will make 10 to 12 wraps, depending on the size of your collard leaves. A 9-inch square baking pan or a 7-by-11-inch casserole dish are good choices for baking. You want the wraps to tuck in next to each other to help hold their form while they bake.

1. Prepare the collared leaves: Bring a large soup pot of salted water to a boil over medium-high heat.

2. Lay a collard leaf flat on a cutting board and slice with your knife flat against the leaf so you thin the stem to be flush with the leaf. Repeat for all leaves.

3. Use a medium bowl to prepare an ice bath of water and ice cubes for the leaves.

4. Use tongs to submerge each collard leaf in the boiling water for 2 minutes. This can be done in batches, a few leaves at a time. Immediately transfer the leaves to the ice bath to cool down for a couple of seconds, and then transfer them to a clean kitchen towel laid out on the counter with the leaf spread open, to absorb the excess water.

5. Prepare the stuffing: Heat the olive oil in a large skillet over medium-high, then add the onion and carrots. Stir occasionally until the onion is translucent and slightly browned, and the carrots are soft, about 5 minutes. Add ½ teaspoon of the salt, ¼ teaspoon of the pepper, and the cardamom, cinnamon, and cumin. Cook for another minute or two until fragrant and golden, then remove the skillet from the heat and transfer its contents to a large bowl.

6. Add the lentils and quinoa to the bowl of cooked vegetables. Add the raisins, lemon zest and juice, dill, mint, and parsley. Stir well. Add the remaining ½ teaspoon of salt and ¼ teaspoon of pepper, or season to taste. Stir again to combine all the ingredients.

7. Preheat the oven to 350°F.

8. Make the stuffed collard greens: Lay a cooled collard leaf flat on a cutting board. Place ¼ to ⅓ cup of stuffing (depending on leaf size) in the middle of the leaf and form into a loose rectangle. Fold in the left and right sides of the collard so that they lay over but don't disturb the stuffing. Pull the

bottom end up and over the filling and roll it into a burrito-style shape.

9. Lay the stuffed collard, seam side down, in a baking dish. Repeat until all collards and stuffing are used up.

10. Brush each collard wrap lightly with olive oil and top with a ½ or ¼ lemon slice. Bake 15 to 20 minutes, until the lemons are slightly charred and the collards are tender. Serve warm or at room temperature.

Acorn Squash and Walnut Galette with Rosemary Honey

SERVES 8

I struggle with intricate, pretty details in baking, so when I first read that galettes were intended to be rustic and imperfect, they quickly became my favorite thing to make. This one is layered with very thinly sliced acorn squash over a cornmeal cookielike crust. Plan ahead for this one because the dough will need to rest for one hour.

Crust

1½ cups (180 g) all-purpose flour

¼ cup (40 g) medium-ground cornmeal

¼ cup light brown sugar

½ teaspoon fine sea salt

8 tablespoons (1 stick) cold unsalted butter, cubed

5 tablespoons whole milk, plus more if needed

Rosemary Honey

3 tablespoons honey

1 tablespoon water

¼ teaspoon minced fresh rosemary

Pinch of fine sea salt

Filling

½ small acorn squash

2 tablespoons finely chopped raw walnuts

1. Make the crust: Place the flour, cornmeal, brown sugar, and salt in a food processor or blender. Pulse a few times to mix. Add the butter and pulse until it is distributed in pea-size pieces. Add the milk, a tablespoon at a time, and continue to pulse until the ingredients come together in a dough ball. You may need to scrape the sides of the bowl or pitcher as you work. The dough ball should be shapeable and not too sticky; add more milk, if necessary, to reach the right consistency.

2. Remove the ball of dough, flatten into a disk, and place in a sealed container in the refrigerator to chill for 1 hour.

3. Meanwhile, make the honey: Stir together the honey and water in a small saucepan. Warm over medium heat, stirring often, about 2 minutes. Remove from the heat. Stir in the rosemary and salt. Set aside.

4. Make the filling: Scrape and discard the seeds from the half squash. Cut the half in two from stem to end. Trim the ends of each piece. Use a mandoline to thinly slice the squash. I like to use setting 2 on my handheld mandoline. You need about 1½ cups of thinly sliced squash.

5. Once the dough has chilled, preheat the oven to 375°F.

6. Place the disk of dough on a piece of parchment paper and lightly flour each side of the disk. Roll to a 10-inch circle.

7. Reserve about a tablespoon of the honey for after baking. Brush the crust with one-third of the remaining honey.

8. Layer your squash slices in a circular pattern on the rolled dough, leaving about an inch bare around the edge of the circle. Sprinkle the walnuts over the squash. Drizzle half of the remaining honey over the squash and walnuts.

9. Fold or roll the dough up around the edge of the galette, creating a crust edge. Brush the remaining honey over the crust edge.

10. Slide the parchment with the galette onto a baking sheet. Bake for 25 minutes, or until the crust is firm and golden brown. Remove from the oven and brush the crust with the reserved honey while the galette is still hot.

11. Serve slightly warm or at room temperature.

Kiwifruit and Pistachio Chia Breakfast Pudding

SERVES 3

It wasn't that long ago I learned that California leads the United States in kiwifruit production. Kiwis grow on vines that reside mostly throughout the Sacramento and San Joaquin valleys, and they are harvested in fall. I love the delicate tartness that the fruit adds to this sweet, creamy pudding. I also think a little ground ginger pairs well with kiwifruit, but I've left that as optional because this pudding is equally good with or without it. Make the pudding and kiwifruit puree just before bedtime and assemble it all in the morning.

One 13.5-ounce can coconut milk

2 tablespoons honey

¼ cup chia seeds

Pinch of fine sea salt

3 kiwifruit, peeled and chopped, plus sliced kiwifruit for serving

¼ teaspoon ground ginger, optional

¼ cup roasted, salted pistachios, chopped

Note: When soaked, chia seeds soften and thicken the liquid that surrounds them. As they sit, they can get a little bit clumpy, so be sure to give the pudding a vigorous stir before you spoon out your servings.

1. Stir together the coconut milk and honey in a medium bowl that has a lid. Continue to stir until the honey dissolves. If you are working with a thick honey, you can always warm it in the microwave about 10 seconds to thin it, but I find that continuous stirring for a minute or so does the job.

2. Add the chia seeds to the coconut milk and honey. Stir well so that they are completely submerged in the liquid. Add the pinch of salt, give it a final stir, secure the lid on the bowl, and refrigerate overnight.

3. Place the chopped kiwifruit in a small food processor, or you can use a bowl and an immersion blender. Add the ginger, if using. Pulse to blend the fruit until it resembles a chunky jam, about 20 seconds. Transfer the fruit puree to a separate bowl with a lid and refrigerate overnight.

4. To assemble the pudding: Spoon some of the chia pudding in each of three serving cups or jars. Then, add some kiwi puree. You can create as many layers as you like, or simply add the pudding to a bowl and top it with the kiwi puree.

5. Sprinkle the top generously with pistachios and add a slice or two of kiwifruit before serving.

CAPAY MILLS

DAVID KAISEL, ESPARTO

Today, California isn't best known for producing large quantities of cereal grains, but that doesn't mean that we don't have resources for local, small-batch, whole-grain flours. David Kaisel is the owner of Capay Mills, a stone flour mill that transforms local heirloom grains into fresh flours.

David's product is flour, but he also has a passion for translating what buying and using these flours made from locally grown, historical grains mean for those he partners with and his customers.

At one point in history, most towns had a small, local mill that processed grains grown in the area to create flours. While that may be difficult to replicate in current times, David believes it is possible to bring local cereal grains back to California consumers. It takes creating a viable business model that benefits everyone in the supply chain from grower to consumer and inspiring appreciation around the quality of the product.

David grows some of his own grains and also sources from other California growers. He focuses on historical varieties and varieties that thrive in the specific microclimate of the Capay Valley. He prioritizes certified organic grains, grains grown without synthetic inputs, and those that are rain fed.

There are five things that make Capay Mills's flours so desirable: flavor, nutrition, agronomic benefits, environmental sustainability, and support of the local economy.

The grains are stone ground, not sifted. They are true whole-grain flours. "When I say whole-grain flours, I mean what goes into the mill comes out of the mill," says David.

Unlike industrial roller mills used to separate

out parts of the wheat, such as the germ, to give flours a lengthy shelf life, stone milling ensures there is bran and germ still in the flour. These components preserve both flavor and nutrients.

David sells to California chefs and artisanal bakers working in establishments that range from Michelin-starred restaurants to celebrated bakeries. But that is just 50 percent of his business. Home bakers buy his flours at Napa Valley farmers' markets and can place orders online.

"I would like for flour to go through the same transformation as wine, chocolate, and coffee," says David. These products have gone from standard commodities to being well understood and appreciated for their history and origins. They've become recognized for flavor profiles and nutritional benefits. He hopes that locally grown and milled flours will continue to gain this same reverence.

Sweet Potato Dinner Rolls with Sage Brown Butter

MAKES 9 ROLLS

These tender dinner rolls are made with Capay Mills Hollis, a hard red spring wheat flour. It's ideal for blending with all-purpose flour and doing so results in a soft roll that has a whole wheat heartiness without the heaviness. The combination of sweet potato puree and honey adds sweetness that meets the nutty, floral sage brown butter with each bite. These rolls are a winner for the holiday table.

**3 tablespoons unsalted butter, plus
   more for pan and bowl**

6 ounces (¾ cup) warm water, 110° to 115°F

1 tablespoon honey

One packet active dry yeast (2¼ teaspoons)

180 g (1½ cups) hard red spring wheat flour

**180 g (1½ cups) all-purpose flour,
   plus more for dusting**

5 fresh sage leaves

1 teaspoon fine sea salt

1 large egg

⅓ cup sweet potato puree

Note: You'll need ⅓ cup of sweet potato puree for this recipe, which I find to be one small sweet potato. I microwave it until soft and then puree it in a bowl with an immersion blender.

1. Butter a 9-inch square pan.

2. Pour the warm water into a small bowl. Stir the honey into the water, then stir in the yeast. Let it sit until the yeast blooms, about 5 minutes. Bubbles will travel to the top and burst into foam that will form on the top of the water. If this doesn't happen, it either means your water was too hot and killed the yeast or your yeast is no longer active; in that case, discard it and repeat with cooler water and new yeast.

3. Combine the flours in the bowl of a stand mixer fitted with the dough hook attachment. Mince three of the sage leaves and add them to the flour.

4. Set the mixer at low speed and pour in the bloomed yeast with the water. Scrape the sides of the bowl as needed and increase the speed to medium. Mix in the salt and then add the egg.

5. Continue to mix until a dry, crumbly dough forms in the center of the bowl, 1 to 2 minutes.

6. Add the sweet potato puree. Increase the mixer speed from medium to medium-high. Continue to mix until a sticky dough ball forms in the bowl. Let the mixer knead the dough for 5 minutes. It will be smooth and slightly sticky.

7. Use floured hands to transfer the dough to a countertop lightly dusted with flour. Knead for 1 to 2 minutes and form into a smooth ball.

8. Lightly coat a large bowl with butter. Place the dough in the bowl. Cover with a clean dish towel and let rest at room temperature until the dough has risen and doubled in size, 1 to 2 hours.

9. Punch down the dough, then knead it back into a ball. Cut it into nine rolls, about 2.6 ounces each.

10. Roll the pieces of dough into balls. Clean surfaces without flour are best for forming rolls because they help the dough to stick and form into a ball.

11. Place the rolls on the prepared pan. Set the pan on the stove and cover with a clean dish towel. Preheat the oven to 375°F and let the rolls proof on the stove for about 20 minutes while the oven preheats.

12. Bake the rolls for 20 minutes, until golden brown and firm.

13. While the rolls bake, melt the 3 tablespoons of butter in a small saucepan over medium heat. Swirl it in the pan as it cooks. The butter will begin to bubble, then the bubbles will turn to foam. Cook for 2 to 3 minutes until brown flecks form at the bottom of the butter and it turns golden yellow to light brown in color.

14. Remove from the heat. Tear the sage leaves in half and place them in the butter. Set the saucepan aside.

15. Once you remove the rolls from the oven, brush them generously with the butter. Discard any large sage leaves. Serve the rolls warm or at room temperature.

Sweet Potato Honey Mustard Salad with Walnuts

SERVES 6

When dining at a local deli while visiting my family many years ago, I encountered a sweet potato salad. The tender pieces of roasted sweet potato were coated in a smooth honey mustard dressing, and it was loaded with chunky walnuts. I've never stopped thinking about it and this recipe is my version of the one I discovered on that visit. I've always felt that sweet potatoes are a hidden gem here in California. While it isn't always the first crop we associate with the state, there are many sweet potato farms, especially in the Central Valley. This recipe is right at home in California, especially when you add local walnuts and incorporate local honey. Sierra Honey Farm (page 94) makes Onion Blossom Honey from bees that have worked fields of onion flowers. It has a delicate savory note that is outstanding in this recipe. If you can't find it, any darker, amber-colored honey will do.

1½ pounds sweet potatoes (about 6 small)

1 tablespoon extra-virgin olive oil

¼ teaspoon fine sea salt

¼ teaspoon ground black pepper

⅔ cup raw walnut halves

Flake sea salt for garnish (optional)

Honey Mustard Dressing

3 tablespoons honey

1 tablespoon Dijon mustard

1 tablespoon spicy brown mustard

1 teaspoon apple cider vinegar

3 tablespoons extra-virgin olive oil

Pinch of fine sea salt

Pinch of ground black pepper

1. Preheat the oven to 425°F and line a baking sheet with parchment paper.

2. Trim the ends of the sweet potatoes and cut them into 1- to 1½-inch pieces. Place them on the prepared baking sheet. Pour the olive oil over them and add the salt and pepper. Stir to coat all the pieces, then spread them out, in a single layer, on the prepared baking sheet.

3. Bake for 15 minutes, or until the edges begin to darken. Stir and bake for 10 to 15 more minutes until fork-tender but not mushy. Remove from the oven and let cool while you toast the walnuts and make the dressing.

4. Place the walnuts in a dry skillet over medium-high heat and toast for 3 to 4 minutes as you toss them in the pan. You'll start to smell the nutty aroma and they will darken only slightly. Set them aside to cool.

5. Make the dressing: Whisk together the honey, Dijon mustard, spicy brown mustard, and apple cider vinegar in a small bowl until smooth. Whisk in the olive oil and then the salt and pepper. Whisk until a smooth, creamy dressing forms, about 1 minute.

6. Once the potatoes have cooled to barely warm, pour the dressing over them and add half of the walnuts. Stir to coat all the pieces in the dressing, then transfer the salad to a serving bowl or platter.

7. Top with the remaining walnuts, and flake sea salt, if desired. Serve slightly warm or at room temperature.

Sweet Potato Crumb Pie

SERVES 8

I enjoy exploring the large variety of sweet potatoes in California, and I like to incorporate more than one in my recipes, as with this pie. For the puree, I use a mix of standard Beauregard sweet potatoes, the dark orange Red Garnet, and a Jersey white sweet potato. Each offers a different texture and sweetness for the pie. That being said, I don't consider the variety absolutely necessary. This recipe will be a winner even only the common orange Beauregard.

Crust

**150 g (1¼ cups) all-purpose flour,
    plus more for dusting**

2 tablespoons sugar

½ teaspoon fine sea salt

8 tablespoons (1 stick) cold unsalted butter, cubed

1½ to 2 ounces cold water

Filling

1½ cups pureed sweet potato (about 2¼ pounds)

½ cup light brown sugar

1 large egg

½ teaspoon ground cinnamon

¼ teaspoon ground ginger

¼ teaspoon freshly grated or ground nutmeg

¼ teaspoon fine sea salt

¼ cup whole milk

Crumb Topping

120 g (1 cup) all-purpose flour

⅓ cup light brown sugar

½ teaspoon fine sea salt

¼ teaspoon ground cinnamon

¼ teaspoon freshly grated or ground nutmeg

8 tablespoons (1 stick) cold unsalted butter, cubed

Note: You can make the puree any way you choose, but pricking the potatoes with a fork and microwaving until tender to be the fastest method. Once they are cool enough to handle, cut them open and scoop the flesh into a bowl. Use an immersion blender or potato masher to blend until smooth.

1. Preheat the oven to 375°F.

2. Make the crust: Combine the flour, sugar, and salt in a medium bowl. Add the butter. Use two knives or a pastry blender to work the butter into the dough until it is evenly distributed in pea-size pieces. Add 1½ ounces of the water and stir until the dough will form into a ball. Add up to ½ ounce more water, if needed. Alternatively, you can pulse the ingredients in a food processor.

3. Dust the dough ball with flour and roll on a well-floured surface into a 13-inch circle. Transfer the dough to a 9½-inch-diameter, deep pie pan. Arrange the dough in the pan and crimp the edges. Place the pie pan in the refrigerator to chill while you work on the filling and topping.

4. Make the filling: Stir together the sweet potato puree and brown sugar in a medium bowl. Stir in the egg until all ingredients are combined. Add the cinnamon, ginger, nutmeg, and salt and stir again. Fold in the milk until the filling is smooth.

5. Make the crumb topping: Place the flour in a medium bowl. Add the brown sugar, salt, cinnamon, and nutmeg. Drop in the cubed butter, then use two knives or a pastry blender to work it into the dry ingredients until the butter is mixed through in both large and small pieces. It should be somewhat dry and crumbly.

6. Remove the crust from the refrigerator. Prick the bottom of the crust a few times with a fork. Pour in the sweet potato filling and spread it evenly on the piecrust. Top the filling with the crumble, covering the pie completely.

7. Bake for 40 to 45 minutes, until the crust is golden brown and the center is firm and doesn't jiggle when the pie is moved.

8. Remove from the oven, let cool to room temperature (at least 1 hour), and serve.

BREAD BIKE BAKERY

SAM DENICOLA AND MATT GAMARRA, SAN LUIS OBISPO

"For us the reason for our existence is community. We support the community, and the community supports us," says Sam DeNicola, co-owner of Bread Bike. He and co-owner Matt Gamarra were local bakers who teamed up for what started as a community-supported bakery whose goods were delivered via bike.

Today, they run the company out of a brick-and-mortar location in San Luis Obispo. Customers can buy directly at the bakery, but they also sell at local farmers' markets, supply wholesale customers, and bring bread to those who still take advantage of their original bike delivery program.

While the community they create through their baked goods extends to the customers who enjoy the end product, it starts with the ingredients used to make them. "Our community begins at the farm," says Sam. They work with three California growers who supply their

grains that they then mill in-house daily for their breads and baked goods.

Their sourdough breads are naturally leavened without the presence of commercial yeast. "It's a living entity that we nurture and maintain every day," says Matt. That sourdough culture is combined with their freshly milled, local grains. They use their fresh whole-meal flour in all their products, from breads to cookies.

Bread Bike values balance in the flavor profiles of its products. "They nourish you and you also enjoy eating them," says Matt. He's especially fond of its 100 percent whole wheat bread that is also made with 100 percent California grains.

Sam is also proud of the 100 percent California-grain bread. Seeing the impact that their business practices and products have on the community makes this fulfilling work for him. Their bread is a tool that creates a connection from the community pizza nights they host at the bakery to the extra bread their delivery drivers take to give away for free.

"The end goal is that we want to create a connection between the farms, our team, and the community. We want to create a clear path and share all those stories," says Sam.

California Whole Wheat Sourdough

MAKES 2 LOAVES

I have to admit that despite California's sourdough bread fame, I didn't have a recipe planned for this book. I've worked in bakeries, and I have a cookbook about breads, but I've never branched out to sourdough for fear I'd neglect my starter due to travel. When Matt and Sam of Bread Bike Bakery (page 78) told me they'd love to share their sourdough recipe, I knew it was an opportunity to not only provide you with a recipe, but also to introduce you to the best sourdough bread I have had. The whole-grain loaves they sell at the bakery have pillowy soft centers and a crust with just the right amount of chewiness. This at-home version is the next best thing to buying a loaf from Bread Bike.

To Feed Your Starter

50 g sourdough starter

100 g warm water

100 g all-purpose flour

Whole Wheat Starter

10 g sourdough starter

35 g warm water

45 g stone-ground hard red wheat flour

Final Dough

80 g whole wheat starter

730 g warm water

620 g stone-ground hard red wheat flour

155 g stone-ground hard white wheat flour

20 g salt

All-purpose flour for dusting

Rice flour for dusting

Notes: You will need a few things for success: a sourdough starter, a kitchen scale, and a Dutch oven or similar pan. Whatever starter you typically use for your sourdough bread works in this recipe. Bread Bike uses a combination of California-grown grains that it mills into flour. The flours listed in this recipe are the types of whole-grain flours the bakery uses, so you can seek them out, but the co-owners also share that you'll get a similar loaf if you choose to make the bread with all of one flour versus a blend of the two types. Because flours vary in weight, forget the standard cup measures on this one and stick with exact weights, using a kitchen scale. I consider it essential for success. All the water you use should be warm, 78° to 82°F. For resting the starter and dough, aim for a warm area as instructed below, but don't worry if you can't hit that temperature. I let mine sit out at about 68°F and had success. Also, plan ahead because baking this loaf is a three-day process that is worth every minute that you put into it.

1. On day one, feed your starter so that it is active and ready to make bread. At about 8 a.m., mix 50 grams of your sourdough starter with 50 grams of warm water and 50 grams of all-purpose flour, in a small bowl. Leave it in a warm area, preferably a little warmer than room temperature, 78° to 82°F.

2. Repeat this process at about noon. Mix 50 grams of the starter you made that morning with 50 grams more of warm water and 50 grams more of all-purpose flour. Leave it again in a warm area.

3. At about 4 p.m. the same day, make the whole wheat starter: Add 10 grams of your sourdough starter that was fed at noon to a separate bowl, stir in the warm water, and then the flour. Let it sit at room temperature overnight.

4. On day two at about 8 a.m., mix the ingredients for the final dough: Stir together the whole wheat

continues . . .

starter with the water. Add the flours and the salt and stir until all the ingredients are combined. Cover the bowl with a clean tea towel and let sit for 45 minutes.

5. Use wet hands to fold the dough over three times in the bowl. Let rest for another 45 minutes. Continue to rest and fold the dough every 45 minutes until it is fermented. It will increase in volume and will appear bubbly on the top. This can take as few as 2½ hours or as long as 4 hours, depending on the temperature of your kitchen.

6. Dump out the dough onto a clean, smooth surface. Use wet hands to divide the dough into two 800-gram pieces and reshape them into rounds. Let them rest, covered with a clean tea towel, for 15 to 20 minutes.

7. Dust the loaves with all-purpose flour and shape each piece of dough into a boule, a round loaf. Dust two proofing baskets with rice flour to prevent the dough from sticking. Place each loaf in a proofing basket.

8. Let the bread proof at room temperature for 15 to 20 minutes before putting them in the refrigerator to rest overnight. You can cover them with a clean tea towel, if desired, but this is not essential.

9. On the morning of day three, remove the loaves from the refrigerator. Place a Dutch oven or cast-iron combo cooker in the oven and preheat it to 500°F. If you only have one Dutch oven or cooker or can only fit one in your oven at a time, you'll need to bake the loaves one at a time. In that case, leave the other loaf in the refrigerator while the first one bakes.

10. Dust the bottom of the loaf with rice flour or cut a small piece of parchment paper the size of the loaf and place it in the bottom of the Dutch oven. This will prevent the loaf from sticking to the bottom.

11. Transfer the loaf from the proofing basket into the Dutch oven, score the top of the loaf with a sharp knife, secure the lid, and place in the oven. Lower the temperature to 450°F.

12. Bake for 20 minutes. Remove the lid and bake for an additional 15 to 20 minutes, until the top is dark golden brown.

13. Remove from the oven and let cool for 1 hour before removing the loaf from the pan. Let it cool thoroughly, about 2 hours, before slicing.

Bread Bike Bakery

CHAPTER 2

FROM THE TREES

I hesitate to pick favorites, but if you forced me to, the foods I'm most fond of in this state are those that come from our trees. For me, they are what makes California such a special place in which to live and cook. Here, you can witness a true tree-to-table experience as the red flowers of a pomegranate tree or the white blossoms of an orange slowly transition into the fruit that makes its way into your kitchen.

California grows 100 percent of the dried figs and 98 percent of the fresh figs sold commercially in the United States. Almonds are in our top 5 of foods produced here, while pistachios and walnuts aren't far behind, falling in the top 10. Our farmers also lead the nation in the production of avocados, dates, persimmons, pomegranates, and stone fruits, such as peaches, nectarines, and pluots.

The oranges, lemons, limes, kumquats, and tangerines grown here reach both local tables and tables in homes across the country. Olives turn into canned table olives, brined olives in a jar, and award-winning olive oils.

The food from our trees gives us the sweet, peppery, crunchy, and tart ingredients that round out classic recipes and put a twist on new creations. The recipes in this chapter take you on an exploration of the food from the trees of California.

Skillet Nectarine and Sweet Corn Salad

MAKES 4 TO 6 SERVINGS

One of my favorite side dishes while growing up was a simple sauté of fresh corn just cut from the cob, with onion and green bell pepper. As I got older and my taste buds grew adventurous, I found myself adding more and more ingredients, building off that simple three-ingredient base. Green bell pepper shifted to a mix of green, red, and yellow. Garlic became essential, along with a fresh herb. Then, I started adding stone fruit, as I do in this recipe. Crisp nectarines, warm in the pan, add an extra bite of sweetness alongside the corn and peppers. It is truly summer in a skillet.

2 tablespoons extra-virgin olive oil

2 garlic cloves, minced

1 medium white onion, diced

1 small green bell pepper, cored and diced

1 small red bell pepper, cored and diced

1 small yellow bell pepper, cored and diced

1 teaspoon fine sea salt, or to taste

½ teaspoon ground black pepper, or to taste

Kernels from 3 ears of corn

½ teaspoon minced fresh rosemary

2 yellow nectarines, pitted and diced

Notes: Other skillets will work, but I always use cast iron for this recipe. Your onion yield should come out to about 1 cup, and your bell peppers to about ¾ cup each, but this is one of those flexible recipes and it doesn't need to be exact.

1. Heat the olive oil in a large skillet over medium-high. Add the garlic and onion. Cook until the onion softens and begins to turn translucent, about 3 minutes.

2. Stir in the green, red, and yellow bell peppers. Cook until they soften on the edges but are still somewhat crisp, about 3 more minutes. Stir in ½ teaspoon of the salt and ¼ teaspoon of the black pepper.

3. Add the corn and rosemary. Cook just until the corn warms through, about 3 more minutes.

4. Add the nectarines and cook until warm, about 2 minutes.

5. Stir in the remaining ½ teaspoon of salt and ¼ teaspoon of black pepper, adjust to taste, and serve warm.

MASUMOTO FAMILY FARM

NIKIKO MASUMOTO, DEL REY

Masumoto Family Farm was founded in 1948 when Nikiko's grandparents bought 40 acres of land south of Fresno in Del Rey. In the late '80s, her father, Mas, began incorporating the organic practices they still use today to produce their highly sought-after apricots, peaches, and nectarines, as well as grapes for raisins.

Nikiko is in her 12th season of farming full time with her father. "Being a farmer is a gift from our ancestors and a promise for the future," she says.

Coming back to the farm to work was not always in Nikiko's plan. "My story of coming back to the farm is wonderfully full of surprises," she says. "I thought success was urban. I would have to leave and not come back to have it."

It was about her second year of college when learning about the impact of pesticide use that things began to change for her. "I didn't understand how important it is, what my family does, until that moment," says Nikiko. At that point, she had made her decision. "The most courageous thing I could do with my life was to come back and farm."

Every summer chefs, breweries, and local families await the organic fruit that comes from their farm. It becomes the star of restaurant summer specials, it gets infused into some of the best beers of California, and of course, it's enjoyed straight from the tree and in family recipes. The stone fruits that are hand-picked at peak ripeness are sold through the drive-thru fruit pickup the farm offers twice per week during harvest season and directly to specialty markets and restaurants.

"We've chosen the varieties we grow based on flavor. We want people to take a bite and say that's the best nectarine I've ever had," says Nikiko. The fruits they grow give people an experience that

creates a lifelong relationship with food. They spark a curiosity that can lead to exploring new flavors and adventures with cooking.

When asked about her favorite variety, Nikiko says, "There is one variety that needs so much more love. The Gold Dust peach." She explains that there is a bias toward large peaches and nectarines. The bigger the better for most consumers. The Gold Dust peach stays small and yellow or gold. It doesn't blush, meaning it doesn't take on that familiar red color of other ripe varieties. "What is special about this variety is that at peak ripeness you can almost peel the skin off like a banana. They are excellent for canning," says Nikiko.

Peach Prosciutto Burrata Grilled Cheese

SERVES 4

This sandwich combines a mix of sweet and savory flavors with creamy and chewy textures, but it doesn't stop there. It's a blend of temperatures, too. The very interior of the burrata stays slightly cool while everything around it is piping hot. This makes four sandwiches, but you can easily double the recipe, or cut it in half, depending on how many you need to serve.

3 tablespoons unsalted butter, softened

8 slices sourdough bread

Two 4-ounce balls burrata, drained and cut in half

6 large fresh basil leaves, sliced or torn

4 ounces prosciutto, chopped

2 small peaches, pitted and sliced

1. Divide the butter and spread it on one side of each of the slices of bread. Heat a large skillet with a lid over medium until warm.

2. For each sandwich, place one slice of bread, butter side down, in the skillet. You can work one sandwich at a time or cook all four sandwiches at once, depending on the size of your skillet and bread slices.

3. Top the slices in the skillet with half of the burrata, cut side up. Spread and tear it gently to cover the bread. Sprinkle each with one-quarter of the basil, 1 ounce of the prosciutto, and one-half sliced peach. Cover the skillet with the lid and let warm for 1 to 2 minutes. The heat should be high enough to lightly toast the bread, but not burn it before the fillings warm up.

4. Place the top slice of bread over the sandwich fillings, butter side up. Use a spatula to gently smash the ingredients inside the sandwich so they will hold together as you flip it.

5. Carefully flip the sandwiches. Cook until the other slice of bread is golden brown on the outside, 2 to 3 minutes.

6. Cut and serve right away while warm.

Apricots with Brie, Almonds, and Honey

MAKES 24

I love making this quick appetizer during apricot season. It takes only a few minutes under the broiler and the result is toasted almonds with velvety smooth Brie over a warm, delicate apricot. The fruit remains a little firm, creating a pleasing blend of flavors and textures. How much honey to add will depend on how sweet your apricots happen to be. If it's early in the season and the apricots are still a little on the tart side, I'm more generous with my honey drizzle.

12 apricots, halved and pitted (about 1½ pounds)
One 8-ounce wheel Brie, cut in 24 pieces
⅓ cup raw almonds, chopped
⅓ to ½ cup honey
Sea salt (optional)

1. Preheat the broiler to 500°F and place the oven rack just one notch above the center level of the oven. It's best not to have it too close to the broiler, so the ingredients have time to warm before the nuts get too toasted. Cover a baking sheet with parchment paper.

2. Arrange the apricots, cut side up, on the prepared baking sheet. Top each with a piece of Brie. Press about 1 teaspoon of almonds into the Brie. Clean up any small pieces that have fallen around the apricots, so they don't burn under the broiler.

3. Place the pan in the oven and watch it closely, until the cheese begins to bubble and melt and the almonds toast. It takes only about 3 minutes, but they can burn quickly.

4. Remove the pan from the oven. Drizzle each apricot with honey. Add a tiny pinch of fine sea salt, if desired, and enjoy warm.

Plumcot Chile Jam

MAKES ABOUT ONE 1-PINT JAR PLUS ONE 4-OUNCE JAR

If I had to pick a favorite jam, this would be it. My mom grew up with her grandmother making plum jam, which I've since learned reflects our German roots. So, I'm not sure whether my love for a jam like this is genetic or simply because it has an appealing balance of sweet and tart character. My version also has a touch of lingering heat that creates a trifecta of flavor. It's sweet enough to top your oatmeal but creative enough to serve with cheeses on a snack board.

I make this jam with plumcots, which are a plum and apricot hybrid. I've also made it with plums. Feel free to take your pick, but it's important to note that there are many varieties of both fruits that range in the color of skin and flesh from deep purple to yellow. If you choose a yellow variety, of course, your jam will be yellow as well. The recipe makes enough for a 1-pint jar for you and a small 4-ounce jar to share.

2 pounds plumcots, pitted and chopped (about 10 large fruit, or 5 cups)

½ cup sugar

1 tablespoon fresh lemon juice (from ½ lemon)

½ to 1 teaspoon crushed Aleppo chile pepper

Note: I love how fruity crushed Aleppo chile pepper complements the plumcots, but you can use crushed red pepper instead. I have a suggested range based on the preferred heat level. For sweeter uses, lean toward a half teaspoon. For savory uses, such as topping cheese and crackers, feel free to lean toward the full teaspoon.

1. Place a small plate in the freezer.

2. Stir together the plumcots, sugar, and lemon juice in a deep, heavy pot set over medium-high heat.

3. Let the contents come to a boil, stirring occasionally. Lower the heat slightly to maintain the boil and cook for 10 minutes, stirring more often the longer it cooks, until the jam thickens.

4. Once you approach 10 minutes, lower the heat to medium-low and test your jam. Remove the plate from the freezer and place a teaspoonful of jam on it. Return it to the freezer for 1 minute. Run your finger through the jam, and if it has firmed to a spreadable consistency, it's ready. If not, return the jam in the pot to a full boil and try the test again in a minute or two.

5. Once the jam has thickened, remove it from the heat and stir in the Aleppo chile pepper.

6. Transfer the jam to a sterilized pint-size jar and a 4-ounce jar. Seal with the lids and store in the refrigerator to use within 5 days.

Stone Fruit Dump Cake

SERVES 6

I grew up with cake mix desserts, such as dump cakes, and while I think that is the worst name to give such an excellent dessert, I still love them. Traditionally, these simple desserts combine pie filling or canned fruit topped with dry cake mix and butter. They're baked into a scoopable dessert that screams "comfort food." With all the fantastic fresh fruit we have in California, it would be a shame to use canned, so in this version I use fresh peaches and nectarines. Cake mix is surprisingly easy to make, so the topping here is homemade, too. You can use all-purpose flour, but I like to use Sonora White heirloom flour from Capay Mills. It's a hard white whole-grain flour and it contributes that delicate graininess that we associate with boxed cake mix.

Fruit

4 cups chopped peaches and nectarines

2 tablespoons sugar

1 tablespoon fresh lemon juice (from ½ lemon)

1 teaspoon pure vanilla extract

Unsalted butter for baking dish

Topping

2 cups (240 g) Sonora White heirloom flour

1 cup sugar

1 teaspoon baking powder

1 teaspoon salt

12 tablespoons (1½ sticks) unsalted butter, cubed

Note: You'll need 4 cups of chopped fruit, which I find ends up being six to eight peaches and nectarines. You can work in other stone fruits, such as cherries and plums, but I do think this dessert is best when there is a tart element. Overall, it's a very sweet dessert and the tartness of a nectarine or a plum skin balances the flavors beautifully.

1. Make the fruit: Combine the chopped fruit in a medium bowl and stir in the sugar, lemon juice, and vanilla. Let sit for 10 to 15 minutes so the fruit can get nice and juicy.

2. Preheat the oven to 350°F. Butter a baking dish that is about 2 quarts in volume.

3. Make the topping: Stir together the flour, sugar, baking powder, and salt in a medium bowl.

4. Spoon the fruit and its juices into the prepared baking dish. Pour the dry topping over the fruit to cover it. Place the cubes of butter over the topping, covering it evenly.

5. Set the baking dish on a baking sheet just in case anything bubbles over while it's baking. Bake for 45 minutes, until the top is golden brown and the fruit is bubbling around the edges. Serve warm or at room temperature.

Nectarine No-Churn Ice Cream

MAKES ABOUT 1½ QUARTS

No-churn ice creams are an easy solution when you want a frozen treat but don't have the time for a hands-on process. The ingredients come together quickly, then it only needs attention once during its freezing time. This ice cream incorporates a simple yellow nectarine jam with cinnamon that is stirred through the cream as it sets up. The result is a silky-smooth treat with tiny bits of seasonal fruit. I like to use Straus Family Creamery Organic Heavy Whipping Cream. I have found that the higher the quality of your cream, the faster it will transform into soft peaks.

1 pint heavy whipping cream

One 14-ounce can sweetened condensed milk

1 yellow nectarine, pitted and diced small

2 tablespoons sugar

2 tablespoons water

¼ teaspoon ground cinnamon

Pinch of fine sea salt

1. Pour the cream into the bowl of a stand mixer fitted with the whisk attachment. Mix on medium speed, then medium-high speed as it thickens, until soft peaks form, about 3 minutes. Alternatively, you can use a hand mixer and a large bowl.

2. Fold in the sweetened condensed milk. Pour it all into a freezer-safe 9-by-5-inch loaf pan. Spread it evenly and freeze for 2 hours, until the edges are firm but it's still soft in the center.

3. While it freezes, combine the nectarine, sugar, and water in a small saucepan over medium-high heat. Bring to a boil, then lower the heat to maintain a low boil, stirring often. Stir constantly as it reaches about 3 minutes of cooking. It will thicken and you can begin to smash the fruit as it cooks. Continue to cook until a thick jam forms, about 5 minutes total.

4. Turn off the heat. Stir in the cinnamon and a small pinch of salt. Transfer the jam to a bowl and place it in the refrigerator while you wait for the ice cream to partially freeze.

5. Remove the ice cream from the freezer and spoon the cooled jam on top, then stir and push the jam into all parts of the soft center of the ice cream so that it is swirled in.

6. Cover the pan with plastic wrap or aluminum foil and return it to the freezer until firm and scoopable, 3 more hours. At this point, it will be firm enough to scoop for serving in bowls. To scoop for cones, let it freeze for 2 more hours.

7. It will keep in the freezer for 5 days, but it's best within a day or two of being made. For better storage, once the ice cream is frozen, press the plastic wrap to make contact with the surface of the ice cream. Then, cover the top securely with aluminum foil.

SIERRA HONEY FARM

THOMAS MCCALL, PASO ROBLES

"To be honest, I never ever, ever thought any of this would happen. I don't know. This is just crazy," says Thomas McCall as he tells me about his company, Sierra Honey Farm. His honey is sold in area stores and celebrated on the menus of local restaurants.

We are standing in an expansive field dotted with the purple flowers of vetch, one of the few wildflowers that produce nectar for honey. This plot of land where Thomas keeps bees is the property of a local winery and part of the company's focus on creating small-crop honey from secluded private ranches along the California Central Coast.

Thomas comes from a family of commercial beekeepers. "When I worked for the family company, my grandpa would say pollination, pollination, pollination. Not honey, because you don't know if you're going to make it or not. That made sense, but times change. I went straight for honey," he says.

Today, Thomas drops somewhere between 32 and 64 hives at each location versus the hundreds of hives dropped by a large commercial beekeeper. Even if it's not the best year, these small numbers ensure the bees will still produce high-quality honey. "I make designer honey, or boutique honey, at each location," he says.

Thomas is constantly exploring new flowers that will produce new flavors in honey. "Every new flower I see, I'll take a picture of it and figure out what it is," he says. He finds fields of drought-tolerant buckwheat hidden in canyons and considers Carmel a magical place for black sage. "What I've learned is purple sage is a little darker. White sage is a little darker. But black sage can be clear as water and it tastes like fruit punch. Pure black sage honey is amazing," he says.

Creating Sierra Honey Farm honey is a process that takes much longer than the time invested in making other honeys. Thomas makes his raw honey using no heat, steam, or separators to extract it, maintaining a higher-quality product. "It's never been about always getting further. It's always going slow and making sure everything is 100 percent. I think that's the right way to do it," he says.

Avocado Banana Salad with Honey Lime Dressing

SERVES 2

A friend and fellow transplant to California once told me, "Well, we live in California. It's a requirement to eat at least half of an avocado a day." While living here does have me incorporating the fruit almost daily, the combination of avocado and banana, along with enjoying avocado in a sweet preparation versus savory, is something I was introduced to while living in Brazil. A simple fruit salad like this one was always offered at the small vegetarian buffet I'd sometimes walk to for lunch. With the abundance of local avocados in so many regions of the state and some farms here, such as Apple Blossom Farms (page 134), growing bananas, it's an easy go-to snack. A honey with deep floral notes, such as Sierra Honey Farm's Super Bloom (page 94), adds something extra special to this fruit salad.

1 avocado, pitted, peeled, and chopped

1 medium banana, sliced

1 tablespoon honey

Juice of 1 lime (2 tablespoons)

Pinch of fine sea salt

Small fresh mint leaves for garnish

1. Arrange the avocado and banana on a serving plate.

2. Stir together the honey, lime juice, and salt in a small bowl. If the honey is thick, place the bowl in the microwave for 10 seconds to warm it just a little. This will help it dissolve into the juice.

3. Pour the dressing over the fruit and garnish with mint leaves. Serve right away as both fruits tend to brown quickly.

Avocado Toast with Radish Sprouts and Walnut Oil

SERVES 1

I wouldn't dare write a California cookbook and not include avocado toast. I eat avocado toast often, both when I'm out and when I make it at home. While there are countless versions served at California cafés, I have a few twists of my own that I haven't encountered elsewhere. Mine always has an egg on top as well as spicy microgreens, such as radish sprouts, to balance the rich avocado. A sprinkle of garlic salt intensifies the savory flavors. Then, I finish it with a drizzle of nutty walnut oil. I often use traditional sourdough bread, but I like to switch it up with a slice from a whole-grain loaf, too. Don't be afraid to experiment with the type of avocado here. At least seven varieties are produced commercially in the state. Hass avocados are nice, but Fuerte and Bacon avocados make great toast, too. This recipe is for one serving of toast, so double or triple as needed.

1 teaspoon olive oil

1 large egg

Pinch of ground black pepper

1 slice bread, toasted

½ avocado, pitted, peeled, and sliced

2 tablespoons microgreens

Pinch of garlic salt

Walnut oil

1. Heat the oil in a small skillet over medium-high. Add the egg and top it with the pepper. Cook to your desired style. I prefer sunny-side up.

2. Place the toast on a serving plate and spread the avocado slices over the top. Add the cooked egg. Top with the microgreens.

3. Sprinkle with a pinch of garlic salt and drizzle with walnut oil. Serve right away.

Avocado Dressed Grilled Corn Salad

SERVES 6

This is my version of a street corn salad with an extra touch of California flavor in the form of avocado dressing. The buttery avocado pairs well with the caramelized edges of corn kernels that have been kissed by the flames of the grill. I love what red onion adds to this salad, but it can also easily overpower it. If you've ended up with a strong, spicy red onion, soak the slices in ice water for about an hour before draining and chopping them finely to top the salad.

6 ears of corn, shucked

1 avocado, pitted and peeled

⅓ cup mayonnaise

Zest of 1 lime

Juice of 1 lime (2 tablespoons)

1 teaspoon Tajín Clásico Seasoning

½ teaspoon fine sea salt

⅓ cup crumbled Cotija, plus more for serving

8 cherry tomatoes, quartered

¼ large red onion, finely chopped

1. Heat a grill to medium-high, about 400°F.

2. Grill the corn until it begins to brown in a few spots, 8 to 10 minutes. Turn it about four times as it cooks, to brown all sides.

3. Once cool enough to handle, cut the kernels from the cob. Place the kernels in a large bowl and discard the cobs. Set aside and let cool to room temperature.

4. Combine the avocado, mayonnaise, half of the lime zest, the lime juice, Tajín, and salt in a small food processor. Blend until a smooth dressing forms, about 30 seconds. Alternatively, you can mash the avocado and stir the ingredients into a dressing with a fork.

5. Pour the dressing over the corn and add the Cotija. Stir well.

6. Transfer to a serving plate or bowl. Top with the cherry tomatoes and red onion. Sprinkle with a little Cotija and the remaining lime zest. Serve right away.

TUDOR RANCH

GEORGE AND JOSEPH TUDOR, MECCA

"When you bite into the date, it's like a bag of honey exploding in your mouth," says George Tudor of Tudor Ranch. He explains that this is why he prefers the earlier-harvested, wet fruit. As a date ages, its flavors tend to deepen from honey to richer molasses. The family-owned and -operated ranch was started by his grandfather in the 1940s. Through his work and that of George's father, brother, and uncle, it has evolved to its location in California's Coachella Valley.

"It's challenging work, but there's also a sense of pride. It's all our family who run it. It's something my grandfather started. My dad would probably be pretty proud that we're still doing it. My mom is always so happy that we can work together and keep it going," says George's brother Joseph. Joseph comes to the farm each summer to help with shipping and marketing for the family during harvest season.

Tudor Ranch grows Medjool dates in addition to table grapes and lemons. Many of us might view this special area of the state as an impossible growing region because it's the desert. "Dates are only grown in one place in the Americas and it's right here in this area," says George. The desert provides year-round sunshine, rare frosts, and historically there has been a good supply of water.

The difference between this area and other growing regions of California is that heat makes everything run at a more rapid pace. "The speed of growing here makes you pay constant attention," says George. While a step in the growing process may take 10 days in our Central Valley, it could happen in 5 days here, so farmers have to be attentive and ready to take action.

Date production is a year-round process. As the green dates begin to ripen, they start to shrivel and turn deep brown. They are bagged on the tree to prevent pests from being attracted to their sweetness. Once fully ripe, the fruit is harvested late summer through autumn.

Brandy Date Shake

SERVES 2

California's Coachella Valley grows roughly 90 percent of the dates consumed in the United States. It's no surprise that a trip to the area introduces you to special things made with the fruit. One of the most popular is the classic date shake. There are many recipes, but it's a blend of dates or date paste with milk and ice cream. And dare I say it gets even better with some spirits? In this twist on the classic, dates are soaked in brandy, then used to create a boozy treat. This shake is rich and sweet, so plan on a small portion. It makes about 12 ounces, so two 6-ounce shakes. Plan ahead because your dates will need to soak in the brandy for at least 2 hours.

6 to 8 dates, pitted and chopped (heaping ½ cup)

¾ cup brandy

1½ cups vanilla bean ice cream

¼ cup whole milk

¼ teaspoon ground cinnamon

Pinch of fine sea salt

Note: For this recipe (and for all date recipes in this book), skip the coated date pieces sold in the baking aisle. Creating a creamy, sweet shake requires pitted dates, such as Medjool or Deglet Noor, often found in the produce section of the supermarket, or if you are as fortunate as I am, at your farmers' market.

1. Place the dates in a pint-size mason jar, pour in the brandy, and seal with the lid. Let sit for 2 to 6 hours. The longer the dates soak, the boozier the shake.

2. When the dates are ready, remove 1 tablespoon of the soaking brandy and transfer it to the pitcher of a blender. Strain the dates and add them to the blender. Discard the rest of the brandy (or strain it and use it for cocktails).

3. Add the ice cream, milk, cinnamon, and salt to the blender. Puree on high speed until smooth and all the dates are finely blended into the shake, about 30 seconds. Serve right away.

Wild Rice with Broccolini, Dates, and Pecans

SERVES 6

My favorite side dishes are those that have it all with grains, vegetables, and a few extras thrown in. It's a bonus when, like this recipe, they cover the full family of flavors from earthy to savory, sweet, and nutty. My favorite part here is using dates. Much like we use a raisin or dried cranberry to add a bit of sweetness to a savory side dish, the date adds that sweetness along with a complex molasses-like richness. Roasted pecans pair well with that complex sweetness. While the nut isn't as strongly associated with the state as dates, there are California pecans grown in our Central Valley.

2 tablespoons extra-virgin olive oil

2 garlic cloves, minced

1 medium yellow onion, diced (about 1 cup)

8 ounces broccolini, chopped fine (about 2 cups)

1 teaspoon minced fresh rosemary

¾ teaspoon fine sea salt, or more to taste

¼ teaspoon ground black pepper

3 cups cooked wild rice

⅓ cup chopped roasted and salted pecans

4 Medjool dates, pitted and chopped

Notes: You'll need 3 cups of cooked wild rice. One cup of uncooked wild rice, cooked according to the package directions, will yield about 3 cups. I like to work with cold dates, for easier chopping. They'll warm and slightly melt into the other ingredients when stirred into the rice.

1. Heat the olive oil in a large, deep skillet over medium-high. Add the garlic and onion. Cook, stirring often, until the onion begins to soften and take on a light golden hue.

2. Stir in the broccolini and then the rosemary, ½ teaspoon of the salt, and the pepper. Cook until the broccolini turns bright green and reaches your desired doneness. I like it to still have a firm crunch; this takes about 3 minutes. You can opt to cook it for 5 minutes, or even 7 minutes if you prefer it completely soft.

3. Lower the heat to low. Stir in the cooked wild rice. Then, add the pecans and dates. Stir all the ingredients and cook for about 1 more minute, until everything is heated through. Add the remaining ¼ teaspoon of salt, or more to taste. Serve warm, but it's also good eaten at room temperature or, I think, chilled.

Fig Tarts with Lemon-Thyme Sugar and Almonds

MAKES 6 TARTS

Fresh fig season requires a tart recipe, even if it is a quick and easy version like this one. Prepared puff pastry makes a convenient base for layering on fig slices and a citrus and herb–infused sugar. What I like about these tarts is that they aren't too sweet. They can be enjoyed as a dessert, as a breakfast, or to accompany a cheese board. I use Mission figs here, but Brown Turkey or Kadota figs would make a fine substitute.

1 tablespoon sugar

½ teaspoon lemon zest

½ teaspoon minced fresh thyme

Pinch of fine sea salt

1 sheet frozen puff pastry, thawed

3 Mission figs, each cut in 4 slices

1 large egg

1 tablespoon water

2 tablespoons toasted sliced almonds, finely chopped

Note: Most frozen puff pastry packs come with two sheets of dough, but you'll only need one for this recipe. Unless you choose to double it, which is easy to do. Be sure the pastry is thawed, but it's easiest to work with if it's still chilled when you cut it.

1. Preheat the oven to 400°F. Line a baking sheet with parchment paper.

2. Mix together the tablespoon of sugar, lemon zest, thyme, and salt in a small bowl. Use clean fingers or a fork to massage the sugar into the zest and herbs to release the oils. Set aside.

3. Lay the puff pastry dough on a flat surface and use a 3½-inch round biscuit or cookie cutter to cut out six circles. Place the circles of dough an equal distance apart on the prepared baking sheet.

4. Place two slices of figs in the center of each circle of dough. Stir together the egg and water in a small bowl to create a pale yellow egg wash. Brush the tarts with the egg wash, coating the dough and the figs. Discard any extra egg wash or use it for another recipe.

5. Sprinkle each tart with lemon-thyme sugar. Then, sprinkle each tart with an equal amount of almonds.

6. Bake for 18 to 20 minutes, until puffed, golden brown, and juices run from the figs. Serve warm or at room temperature.

THE SPECIALTY CROP COMPANY AND HERMAN PRODUCE SALES

KEVIN AND ERIK HERMAN, MADERA

Kevin Herman grew up in Kerman, a small town west of Fresno where his parents and grandparents grew raisin grapes. While studying at Fresno State, Kevin was working for a company that was planting fig trees in Madera, and that's what led him to start his own company growing figs and other produce in California's Central Valley.

When asked which fig varieties he grows, Kevin says, "We do a little bit of everything." His company grows Sierra, Mission, Brown Turkey, Conadria, Kadota, and Panache Tiger figs. His orchards produce both fresh and dried figs.

Figs stand out from other fruits, such as raisins, for Kevin because they aren't all the same. "What I like about figs is that each variety has its own flavor profile," he says. He describes himself as a bit of a wine geek, and he encourages people to think about figs and their flavor profiles in the same way they would consider which wine to drink.

For example, the Tiger Fig, with its green and yellow striped exterior, has a bright pink interior. "It almost tastes more like a raspberry than a fig," says Kevin. "Missions have a musky, savory flavor, while Sierras are buttery like chardonnay," he adds.

Their figs can be found around the country through his son Erik's company, Herman Produce Sales. "I've been around figs my whole life," says Erik. He remembers his first job was packing figs as a kid, but his family had never distributed their figs on their own until he started his company. When it comes to varieties, his favorite is, hands down, the Black Mission fig. "People ask me all the time, which is my favorite, which

is sweeter. The Tiger fig looks a lot cooler, but there's something about the Black Mission. You can't beat it," he says.

Fresh fig season varies a little each year, but most often you can find Mission and Brown Turkey from early summer through fall. Some varieties, such as the Tiger Fig, don't come on until August and last only six to eight weeks. Dried figs can be found and enjoyed year-round.

"I encourage people to experiment with both fresh and dried figs and the different varieties,"

says Kevin. He adds that a good place to start is by making the age-old recipe of a fresh fig wrapped in prosciutto and grilled, then drizzled with balsamic vinegar. "This lends well to the Mission fig because of its savory flavors," he says.

Erik enjoys seeing how people cook with figs. Unlike other fruits, they encourage inventive culinary creations. "A fig can be consumed in so many different ways. There are multiple uses for them," says Erik.

Salted Chocolate Fig Smoothie

SERVES 2 TO 3

My secret ingredient in all smoothies is a generous pinch of salt. There is something about a supersweet drink that makes my taste buds crave the balance it creates. In this smoothie, I take things one step further, blending salt with the bitterness of cocoa, the earthiness of fresh Mission figs, and the sweetness of bananas and honey. It hits the spot for those of us who want a quick breakfast smoothie, but who also aren't fans of the traditional berry and yogurt blend. You can make this with fresh bananas, but I always prefer to use frozen for a thicker drink.

1½ cups unsweetened vanilla almond milk

4 fresh Mission figs, stemmed and halved

2 medium frozen bananas

3 tablespoons unsweetened cocoa powder

2 teaspoons honey

¾ teaspoon fine sea salt

Fig slices for serving (optional)

Combine all the ingredients, except the optional fig slices, in the pitcher of a blender. Blend on low speed, then increase the speed to high and puree for 30 seconds, or until everything is blended with no visible pieces of fig skin or frozen banana chunks. Serve right away with half a fig slice, if desired.

Grilled Olive and Cherry Salad

SERVES 4 TO 6

Olives are grown throughout our Central Valley, both for eating and for making oil. The olives we eat are called table olives, but there is a further distinction for the buttery, nutty olives that are canned versus those in brine that often top your martini. Canned olives are California Ripe Olives, and they are still cured using a method created by Freda Ehmann in the 1800s. It's a delightful account to read if you are into culinary history. These olives are my favorite snack and the variety I turn to when cooking. In this salad, their buttery flavor blends with sweet cherries and creamy pearls of mozzarella with a punch of bright, aromatic rosemary.

1 pound sweet cherries, stemmed and pitted

One 6-ounce can green table olives, drained

Cooking oil for grill (optional)

One 8-ounce container mozzarella pearls, drained

1 tablespoon extra-virgin olive oil

1 teaspoon minced fresh rosemary

½ teaspoon flake sea salt

Note: You'll need either metal grilling skewers or soaked wood skewers for this recipe.

1. Heat the grill to high heat, 400°F. Skewer all the cherries and olives. If your grill isn't well seasoned, you can wipe the grates with cooking oil to prevent the fruit from sticking.

2. Grill the skewers for 5 minutes, until there are grill marks on the cherries and the olives blister in a few places. Flip and grill for 5 more minutes.

3. Transfer the warm cherries and olives to a bowl. Stir in the mozzarella pearls, olive oil, rosemary, and salt. Serve right away.

OLIVAIA OLIVE RANCH

RACHELLE BROSS AND GIULIO ZAVOLTA, LINDSAY

"We made it a mission to save the trees," says Giulio Zavolta. He and his wife, Rachelle Bross, bought what is now known as Olivaia Olive Ranch over 10 years ago. The land was at risk for being sold and the olive trees being uprooted and replaced with almond and citrus trees, but Giulio and Rachelle recognized that half of the olive trees on the property are over 125 years old. They knew it was something special.

The first goal they accomplished was regaining relationships within the table olive industry and selling table olives back to Musco Family Olive Co. for the production of California Ripe Olives.

In the process, they discovered that they had a lot of trees that were not Manzanilla or Sevillano, the olives most often grown for table olives. "It turned out that, after we did DNA testing on all these trees, we have 10 unidentified different cultivars of olives and it's from those that we originally started to make our olive oil," says Rachelle.

They began sharing the oil with family and friends, but soon decided it was far too good to keep to themselves. "We thought there's something special here and we really want to share this with the rest of California," says Rachelle. So, in 2017, they launched Olivaia OLA extra-virgin olive oil. OLA stands for Original Lindsay Artisanal due to the history of the trees, the area the oil comes from, and how it is made.

All the olives are hand harvested. "By the time our olives go to the mill, none of them have bruises," says Giulio. "We pride ourselves on making sure we are sending pristine olives to the mill. We also pride ourselves in making sure that our ground here is completely alive."

They keep a ground cover throughout the property, something that is uncommon for the area. They note that making these changes has brought much more wildlife to the property, from birds to frogs. "If you just sit here really quietly, you realize how different it is from before, how alive it sounds. And I think that has absolutely contributed to the oil's flavor," says Rachelle.

Rachelle holds a PhD in nutrition and she's a registered dietitian, so creating this oil is a merging of her passions for food, health, science, and cooking. The versatility and depth of flavor of their oils make them ideal for finishing dishes, but they are also for cooking. "We do everything with our oil," says Rachelle. "Including baking," says Giulio.

"We really believe that oil is a flavor enhancer. It's not just a fat that you add to what you are making. It's there to enhance, to pair, to create magic," he says.

Pistachio Flatbread with Red Grapes

SERVES 2 TO 4

Pistachios are my favorite tree nut grown in the state, not just for their color and flavor, but also because of how they cluster in beautiful bunches on trees. They make an excellent addition to flatbreads and pizzas with white sauce. I use crème fraîche as the sauce here, then top it with cheeses, pistachios, and sliced red table grapes, another ingredient we're well known for here in California. Instead of always making my own dough, I like to seek out local restaurants and bakeries that sell their unbaked dough balls. It's another great way for those of us who enjoy cooking at home to support others who feed us in our communities.

2 tablespoons extra-virgin olive oil, plus more for pan

½ teaspoon minced fresh rosemary

1 pound prepared pizza dough

¼ cup crème fraîche

4 ounces whole-milk mozzarella, chopped

1 ounce freshly grated Parmesan (about ⅓ cup)

¼ small red onion, thinly sliced

½ cup seedless red grapes, sliced

½ cup shelled, salted pistachios, finely chopped

1. Heat the 2 tablespoons of olive oil in a small saucepan over medium-high for 2 minutes. Remove from the heat and add the rosemary. It will sizzle a little when it hits the oil. Set aside to cool.

2. Preheat the oven to 450°F.

3. Roll the pizza dough into a 12-inch circle. Oil a round pizza pan with olive oil. Place the dough on the prepared pan.

4. Reserve 1 tablespoon of the rosemary-infused olive oil from the saucepan. Brush the remaining rosemary oil over the pizza dough. Spread the crème fraîche evenly over the dough, leaving ¼ to ½ inch of crust bare around the edge of the pizza. Top with the mozzarella and the Parmesan. Layer the red onion over the pizza and then scatter with the grape slices. Top with half of the pistachios.

5. Bake for 12 to 15 minutes, until the crust of the flatbread is golden brown and the cheese is browned and bubbling. Remove from the oven, let cool for 5 minutes, then drizzle with the reserved rosemary oil. Cut the pizza into eight slices and serve warm with the remaining pistachios on the side for topping the slices, if desired.

Roasted Olives with Pearl Onions

SERVES 6 TO 8

If all bar snacks were like this, I would probably go out more often. Colorful, bite-size pearl onions are roasted until tender and then fruity black and green olives are added to the mix. Lemon slices give it a tangy glaze. I like to use a light, but grassy and fresh, olive oil like Olivaia's Estate Sevillano EVOO. This snack is best eaten bite by bite with toothpicks while sipping a hazy IPA.

8 ounces assorted pearl onions, peeled

1 small lemon, halved and sliced

1 tablespoon extra-virgin olive oil,
    plus more for serving

¼ teaspoon fine sea salt

One 6-ounce can large black pitted olives, drained

One 6-ounce can medium pitted
    green olives, drained

¼ teaspoon flake sea salt

¼ teaspoon ground black pepper

1. Preheat the oven to 400°F. Line a baking sheet with parchment paper.

2. Spread the onions and lemon slices on the prepared baking sheet. Drizzle with the tablespoon of oil and sprinkle with the salt. Stir gently to combine, then spread back into a single layer.

3. Bake for 15 minutes, until the onions begin to brown and become tender.

4. Add the olives to the baking sheet and give everything a quick stir to combine. Bake for 5 more minutes, until the olives are warmed.

5. Transfer everything to a serving bowl. Sprinkle with the flake sea salt and pepper, and drizzle with some more olive oil. Serve warm or at room temperature.

Walnut Lentil Soup

SERVES 4 AS A STARTER

More than 99 percent of the walnuts grown in the United States come from right here in California, and one way I like to use them is to puree them into soups. Walnuts add a creaminess to legume-based soups and this one is smooth, savory, and extremely simple to make. Since it has such a neutral brown color, a few sprigs of microgreens sprinkled on just before serving make an attractive garnish and provide an extra touch of fresh flavor.

1½ cups dried brown or green lentils, rinsed

5 cups chicken stock, plus more for serving

3 garlic cloves, peeled

Two 2-inch thyme sprigs

One 2-inch rosemary sprig

¼ cup chopped raw walnuts, plus more for garnish

½ teaspoon fine sea salt

Microgreens for serving

Note: If served right away, the soup is at the right creamy, consistency. Once it cools, it will thicken. If you will be eating it later, keep about 1 cup of additional chicken stock on hand to reheat with the soup and then salt it to taste.

1. Combine the lentils and stock in a small soup pot over medium-high heat. Add the garlic cloves and herb sprigs to the pot. The thyme and rosemary sprigs can be added individually, or you can tie them together with kitchen string.

2. Bring to a boil, stirring occasionally to keep any lentils from sticking to the bottom of the pot. Lower the heat to maintain a strong simmer with the pot partially covered. Cook until the lentils and garlic are soft, about 20 minutes. Remove the pot from the heat and discard the herb stems.

3. Stir in the ¼ cup of walnuts and salt. To puree the soup, you can use an immersion blender directly in the pot or transfer the soup to a blender. Puree on high speed until smooth, about 30 seconds. Transfer the soup to serving bowls and garnish with chopped walnuts and microgreens.

MARK HEUER FARMS

MARK AND BETH HEUER, STRATHMORE

Nut trees grow from the far north to the deep south of California's Central Valley. If you happen to be driving down the rural roads of the small town of Strathmore, chances are that some of the almond trees you see belong to Mark Heuer and his family.

"We're a big-size small farm, is how I like to say it," says Mark. He and his brother have farmed in California for 40 years, but the roots of the family lie in northern Germany. The Heuer family farm there began in 1822 and is now run by his cousins.

Mark's dad immigrated to the United States in 1951 and Heuer Farms here in California grow almonds along with a variety of other crops, such as pistachios, olives, grapes for raisins, and oranges. The almonds from their farm are exported around the world.

There are numerous varieties of almonds grown in California, but the Nonpareil is a popular choice. From a culinary perspective, it's one of the top varieties to grow and has been for a long time. Mark explains that it is grown for its size and slicing ability, and he adds that it's a good-tasting nut. While the Nonpareil offers size, texture, and flavors that most of us are accustomed to with almonds, the culinary-minded may want to experiment. "If you like a more flavorful nut, the Fritz is known for its stronger amaretto flavor," he says.

Almonds are a crop that strongly reflects the family's German roots. "Germans have long used almonds, specifically in marzipan," says Mark. His family celebrates the holidays every year with their mother's Marzipan Bread (page 115), which is stuffed with sweet marzipan made by blending almond paste and sugar.

Heuer Family Marzipan Bread

MAKES 2 LOAVES

Not long after I met with Mark and his wife, Beth, Mark's sister Tina followed up with me regarding this recipe. "It's just not Christmas without marzipan bread," Mark had told me. Their mother taught Tina how to make the bread many years ago and it is a family favorite. It has been adapted and refined from a combination of other recipes, such as the bread dough that originated in the *Betty Crocker Cookbook*. The recipe was shared with me in separate parts, some with instructions and not measurements, because it's a recipe that resides in the head and heart, not all in one place on paper. "Bread making is something you just learn to do many times without following a recipe," says Tina. This recipe is compiled from what the family shared with me for how to make the bread. After making it myself, I can see why they love it. I just might make baking it each year a tradition of my own.

Bread

½ cup whole milk

½ cup warm water (110° to 115°F)

Two packets active dry yeast (4½ teaspoons)

½ cup sugar

1 teaspoon salt

2 large eggs

8 tablespoons (1 stick) unsalted butter, softened, plus more for rising bowl and baking sheet

4½ to 5 cups (540 to 600 g) all-purpose flour, plus more for dusting

Marzipan Filling

1 cup almond paste

4 tablespoons (½ stick) unsalted butter, softened

¼ cup sugar

Glaze

2 cups confectioners' sugar

½ teaspoon pure almond extract

8 teaspoons whole milk, plus more as needed

Note: Shared below is the original amount of marzipan filling for the recipe, but Tina tells me she often doubles it.

1. Start the bread: Pour the milk into a medium saucepan and scald it over medium heat. Stir the milk until tiny bubbles begin to form around the outside edge, about 2 minutes. Remove from the heat and let cool to lukewarm, at least 10 minutes.

2. Pour the warm water into the bowl of a stand mixer fitted with the paddle attachment. Dissolve the yeast in the water.

3. Mix in the milk, sugar, salt, eggs, and butter on low speed. Add 2½ cups of the flour. Turn the mixer speed to medium and then to medium-high to beat the mixture until smooth, 1 to 2 minutes.

4. Add the rest of the flour, about ½ cup at a time, with the mixer on low speed, until a dough forms that is soft but not too sticky to handle. It should be firm enough to knead.

5. Transfer the dough to a lightly floured countertop and knead until smooth, elastic, and shapeable, about 5 minutes. Shape into a round loaf.

6. Butter a large bowl and place the round loaf in the bowl. Flip the dough ball once so that the bottom that had initial contact with the buttered bowl is facing up.

7. Cover with a clean dish towel and let rise in a warm place until doubled in size, 1½ to 2 hours. The rise time will depend on the ambient temperature.

8. While the dough rises, make the marzipan filling: Combine the almond paste, butter, and sugar in the clean bowl of the stand mixer fitted with the paddle

continues . . .

attachment. Beat it on medium and then medium-high speed, until it is mixed well and there are no streaks of butter, about 1 minute.

9. Punch down the dough. Then, knead it back into a ball and cut the dough into two equal pieces.

10. Roll each half into a rectangle that is about 9 by 18 inches.

11. Divide the almond paste in half and place it by the spoonful over the rectangles of dough. Spread them a little to cover as much of the rectangle as possible, leaving about an inch around the edge. Roll the dough lengthwise over the marzipan filling, like rolling a cinnamon roll. Press to seal the edge and crimp the ends to seal them, creating a log shape.

12. Place the two loaves, seam side down, on a baking sheet greased with butter and shape the logs into crescents. Use a sharp knife to make about eight slits along the outside of the crescents from the center to the edge, cutting about one-quarter of the way into the loaf. Don't cut all the way through the loaf.

13. Let the bread rest in a warm spot until it doubles in size again, about 1 hour.

14. As the loaves approach the end of the second rise, preheat the oven to 375°F.

15. Bake the bread for 20 to 25 minutes, until the surface is golden brown. Remove from the oven and transfer the loaves to a cooling rack to cool completely, at least 1 hour.

16. Make the glaze: Stir together the confectioners' sugar and almond extract in a small bowl. Add half of the milk and stir until smooth. Continue to add the milk about a teaspoon at a time until a smooth glaze forms. It should be thin enough to drizzle over the bread, but thick enough that it coats the loaves while dripping over the sides.

17. Set the cooling rack with the cooled loaves of bread over the baking sheet and generously pour the glaze over the loaves. You can leave the glaze as a drizzle or use a spoon to spread it to coat each whole loaf. Let the glaze set, about 30 minutes, before slicing to serve. The bread can be wrapped tightly and frozen, but it's best enjoyed within a few weeks.

Mark Heuer Farms

Pomegranate Grain Salad with Walnuts

SERVES 6

As autumn approaches, I can't wait to start finding pomegranates at our local markets. Pomegranate seeds are called arils and they add a juicy bite and tiny crunch to any dish. While they are fresh, and not dried, I like to use them in recipes the same way as you would dried cranberries or raisins. Cold grain salads made with hearty, chewy grains, such as farro, make a nice partner for the sweet burst of juice from the pomegranate. This easy salad blends the grains and arils with crunchy walnuts, another food that is plentiful from the trees in California. This whole-grain side dish can be paired with all types of roasted meats. When I want to add an extra layer of flavor, I top it with some crumbled feta or blue cheese.

1½ cups uncooked farro, cooked according to package directions

1 cup pomegranate arils

3 tablespoons extra-virgin olive oil

1 tablespoon minced shallot

1 teaspoon unseasoned rice vinegar

½ teaspoon fine sea salt, plus more to taste

¼ teaspoon ground black pepper, plus more to taste

¼ teaspoon minced fresh rosemary

⅓ cup chopped raw walnut pieces, toasted

Note: To toast your walnuts, simply place them in a small, dry skillet and cook over medium to medium-high heat, tossing them in the pan until they darken slightly and become fragrant, about 5 minutes.

1. Place the cooled, cooked farro in a large bowl and add the arils. Pour in the olive oil, then add the shallot, vinegar, salt, pepper, and rosemary and stir well. Sprinkle in the walnuts, then stir again.

2. Serve right away. You can refrigerate the salad for up to 8 hours before serving, but wait to add the walnuts until you pull it out of the refrigerator, so that they stay crunchy. Add more salt or pepper to taste when serving.

Fresh Pomegranate Orange Juice

MAKES 16 OUNCES

Pomegranates tend to be messy, especially if you burst the arils to create a juice. Instead of mashing the pomegranate, I find that putting the arils in a blender and then draining the pulp results in a delicious juice that's a lot less of a hassle to make. To mellow out the somewhat tart taste of the pomegranate, I like to add some fresh navel orange juice to sweeten things up.

5 cups pomegranate arils (from 2 extra-large pomegranates)

½ cup navel orange juice (from 2 medium oranges)

1. Combine the pomegranate arils and orange juice in a blender. Puree on high speed for 30 seconds.

2. Place a mesh colander over a large bowl. Pour the contents of the blender into the colander. Let the juice drain for at least 30 minutes. Gently stir the pulp to extract juice a few times as it drains. Discard the pulp.

3. Chill the juice for at least 30 minutes before serving. Although it's best fresh, just after chilling, the juice can be stored in the refrigerator for up to 2 days.

BLOSSOM BLUFF ORCHARDS

BRYCE LOEWEN, PARLIER

Blossom Bluff Orchards first caught my attention for its persimmons and pomegranates. I soon learned that Bryce Loewen, who owns the farm with his sister and his parents, has about 150 different varieties of fruit trees on the farm that range from stone fruits to citrus.

Bryce's great-grandparents emigrated from Germany in the early 1900s and worked as field laborers on local farms until they saved up enough to buy the 30-acre plot that still makes up part of the orchard today.

In the early '90s, Bryce's father got involved in the family farm and began to move production away from conventional methods and toward organic. Bryce says, "It [the decision] was more environmentally based. Organic wasn't really a hip, popular, or high-value thing at the time. It was more about us growing up on the farm having to breathe the air and play in the dirt here."

While today, it's easy to find effective organic resources and a supportive community, at that time of their transition, these weren't widely available. "It took some courage on his part to roll the dice and see what worked," says Bryce.

It turns out that the demand for organic and local farmers' markets started to explode rather quickly after their transition, so that environmentally based decision soon became a wise economic move as well.

The decision to diversify the farm with smaller blocks and more varieties was driven by its selling direct to consumer through farmers' markets. "Having a nice full display all through the summer is crucial. And we have to find things that other people aren't growing. Older varieties, but also newer varieties. Things that are unique," says Bryce.

He got his start working for the farm by helping with farmers' market sales while he was living in the Bay Area. In 2008, he made the decision to move back to the farm and learn how to do the "real work."

"The Central Valley, in general, is a remarkably great place to grow pretty much everything. Our climate, our soil. Maintaining that soil integrity, in my opinion, that's the terroir. The real flavor is coming from the earth," says Bryce.

Because the farm manages its own distribution, it is growing and harvesting on demand. "This means we have the luxury of waiting until the fruit is really, really good because we're planning to pick it and get it to the consumer fast," Bryce says. Letting fruit ripen on the tree gives it more flavor and gives those of us eating it a more unique experience. This allows for that extra level of quality that Blossom Bluff Orchards has become known for.

Grandma Elsie's World-Famous Persimmon Cookies

MAKES ABOUT 3 DOZEN COOKIES

The Hachiya persimmon ranks for me as one of the world's most interesting fruits. That's because it's not ready to eat until it reaches a state when you are sure you should throw it away. As it ripens on your countertop, it will turn from being firm and bright orange to being dotted with soft black patches and a shriveled skin. This is when the pulp inside becomes a sweet jam. It can be scooped out and eaten with a spoon or used in cookies, such as in this family recipe that Bryce at Blossom Bluff Orchards shares with us here.

From the recipe: Start with completely ripe Hachiya persimmons. You'll know they are ready to use when they are almost too soft to pick up without breaking open. They should be translucent, and the pulp should have the consistency of jam. If it looks like they won't be ready by the time you want to use them, you can force Hachiyas to ripen by freezing them.

1 cup Hachiya persimmon pulp

1 cup sugar

8 tablespoons (1 stick) unsalted butter, softened, plus more for pan (optional)

1 teaspoon baking soda

1 large egg, beaten

2 cups (240 g) all-purpose flour

1 teaspoon ground cinnamon

½ teaspoon ground cloves

½ teaspoon ground nutmeg

½ teaspoon salt

1 cup raisins

1 cup chopped raw walnuts

1. Preheat the oven to 375°F. Butter a baking sheet or line it with parchment paper.

2. Beat the persimmon pulp, sugar, butter, and baking soda in a large bowl until creamy, about 3 minutes. Fold in the egg until all ingredients are blended.

3. Fold in the flour, cinnamon, cloves, nutmeg, and salt just until the flour is incorporated into the cookie dough. Fold in the raisins and walnuts.

4. Drop by the spoonful an equal distance apart on the prepared baking sheet, 12 cookies per pan. Bake for 12 to 15 minutes, until the cookies are golden brown and the centers are firm. Remove from the oven and let cool completely before serving.

Blossom Bluff Orchards

Fuyu Persimmon Jicama Slaw

SERVES ABOUT 4

Persimmons can be a mystery to those unfamiliar with them, simply because many people aren't sure what to make with the fruit. Fuyu persimmons have a round but flat, squatty shape and a firm, crisp texture. Many use them in baked goods, but I prefer to treat them the same way you would another crunchy fruit, such as an apple or a pear. In this recipe, I use persimmon slices to sweeten a crunchy jicama slaw with a simple dressing. It's a winner for autumn picnics when the fruit is in season.

1 large jicama, peeled and julienned (about 3 cups)

2 Fuyu persimmons, julienned (about 1½ cups)

2 leaves curly-leaf kale, finely chopped (about ½ cup)

2 tablespoons mayonnaise

2 teaspoons unseasoned rice vinegar

2 teaspoons honey

½ teaspoon fine sea salt

¼ teaspoon ground black pepper

1. Combine the jicama, persimmons, and kale in a medium bowl.

2. For the dressing, stir together the mayonnaise, rice vinegar, honey, salt, and pepper in a small bowl until smooth. Pour the dressing over the slaw and mix to coat well.

3. Serve right away or refrigerate for up to 1 hour before serving.

HEMLY CIDER

SARAH HEMLY, COURTLAND

The rim of a can of Hemly Pear Cider reads, "Estate Grown Since 1850." Not only is a product that dates back that far rare in this state, but it's also rare to find an orchard like Hemly's anywhere else in California.

In the 1800s, pears were planted here, an area referred to as the Delta, because before levees were built, the land would often flood. "Pears are one of the few trees that can handle submersion," says Sarah Hemly.

Sarah and her husband, Matt, a sixth-generation pear farmer, created Hemly Cider using fruits from the orchard his family has owned since 1850. Trees from that time period still exist on the property.

The age of the trees and the terroir of the land give the pears their distinct flavors. "The quality of the fruit in the Delta can't be replicated anywhere else," says Sarah. "I decided I was going to find a way to showcase this fruit."

They traveled to study ciders in Europe but didn't find what they were looking for until a visit to Tasmania. There, they learned about the techniques and practices needed to transform dessert fruit, such as the Bartlett and Bosc pears they grow in the orchard, into a high-quality pear cider.

"We do ciders differently than other cideries in the United States," says Sarah. The fruit matters, it's respected in their process, and the flavors they create come from freshly pressed juices they blend in without additives.

Perry, the traditional name for a pear cider, lacks the acidity often found in apple ciders as well as in beers and wine. Thanks to this lack of acidity, there are few foods, if any, that you can't pair with a pear cider. "Pear is so delicate, it elevates so many different cuisines," Sarah says. Her personal favorites are serving their jalapeño-infused cider with tacos or grilled meats.

Unlike apples, pears are a fruit that is picked green and ripens off the tree. "There's nothing like a ripe Bartlett," says Sarah. "You can feel the ripeness biting into it, and it melts in your mouth. We try to can that perfection for you in our cider."

Hemly Pear Thanksgiving Dressing

SERVES 6 TO 8

I'm one of those people who believes that a Thanks-giving feast is all about the side dishes. So, I'm thrilled that Hemly Cider and Chef Rachael Levine are sharing their version of my favorite side dish, the dressing, for you here. It's studded with the same sweet Hemly pears that make its ciders and it's full of seasonal herbs. Chef Rachael notes that you can save time, the day you prepare your feast, by cutting your bread cubes up to a week in advance and storing them at room temperature. The dressing can also be assembled a day ahead and kept in the refrigerator. Just allow it to approach room tempera-ture before baking, to avoid extra time in the oven.

8 cups sourdough or French sweet bread cubes (from about a 1-pound loaf)

2 tablespoons olive oil

1 cup yellow onion, diced

¾ cup diced celery

1½ cups Bartlett or Bosc pears, cored and diced

¼ cup chiffonaded fresh sage (about 12 leaves)

¼ cup chiffonaded fresh parsley

2 tablespoons fresh thyme

1 teaspoon fine sea salt

½ teaspoon freshly ground black pepper

3 cups chicken or vegetable stock

1. Preheat the oven to 350°F.

2. Spread the bread cubes on a baking sheet and bake for 8 minutes. Stir and bake for another 6 to 8 minutes, until the cubes are dry and toasted on all sides. Place the toasted bread cubes in a large bowl.

3. Heat the olive oil in a large saucepan over medium. Add the onion and celery and cook for 4 to 5 minutes, stirring occasionally, until softened. Add the pears, sage, parsley, and thyme and cook an additional 3 to 4 minutes, until the pears begin to soften.

4. Scrape the mixture from the saucepan and pour over the bread cubes in the bowl. Add the salt and pepper, then toss together. Transfer the contents of the bowl to a casserole dish large enough to hold it all. A 9-by-13-inch casserole dish or baking pan works well, but a slightly smaller dish will result in a deeper layer of stuffing.

5. Pour the stock evenly over the mixture in the cas-serole dish. Let stand for at least 30 minutes prior to baking.

6. While the dressing rests, preheat the oven to 375°F.

7. Cover the dish with aluminum foil. Bake for 40 minutes. Remove the foil and bake for an addi-tional 10 to 15 minutes, until the top is golden brown. Serve warm.

Chef Rachael Levine for Hemly Cider

Candied Walnut, Citrus, and Fennel Salad

SERVES 2 TO 4

This salad is nearly equal parts crunch from candy-coated walnuts, juicy from oranges, and earthy from thinly sliced fennel. It fills the mouth with not only three well-paired flavors, but three textures as well. I use a mandoline to slice the fennel, and I like to divide the bulb and slice each half on a different setting. The first to shave it and the next half just a little thicker. I like the look of supremed oranges, but it's a lot of work. The nutritionist in me justifies simply chopping orange segments because we get some extra nutrients from the albedo (that white fiber between fruit segments). Walnut oil is used to dress this salad, adding to its deep nutty flavors. Be sure to select an unrefined, cold-pressed finishing walnut oil for the best flavor. It doesn't seem like a lot in the recipe, but you'll find the oil has an intensity that flows through the whole salad. I use La Tourangelle Roasted Walnut Oil, but there are other producers of California walnut oil in the state.

2 tablespoons sugar

¼ teaspoon plus a pinch of fine sea salt

½ cup raw walnut halves and pieces

1 medium fennel bulb, thinly sliced

½ tablespoon roasted walnut oil

1 cara orange, peeled and chopped

1 navel orange, peeled and chopped

Fennel fronds for garnish

1. Combine the sugar with the pinch of salt in a small skillet over medium-high heat. Stir the sugar until it begins to melt, about 2 minutes. Work quickly and add the walnuts while lowering the heat to medium. Stir the nuts constantly until the sugar starts to brown. Remove from the heat and continue to stir until all the sugar is dissolved and coats the walnuts. Set aside to cool.

2. Place the fennel in a medium bowl and toss with the walnut oil and the remaining ¼ teaspoon of salt. Layer it on a serving plate. Scatter the orange pieces over the fennel. Break up the cooled walnuts and layer them over the oranges. Garnish the top with fennel fronds and serve.

Homemade Orange Julius

SERVES 3 TO 4

I had no idea that an Orange Julius wasn't one of my mom's original creations until I was well into my teens. It turns out the drink was created in the 1920s in Los Angeles. While many people now know of it due to the chain restaurant that holds the name, back in Indiana in the '80s, we somehow managed to have this California-based drink at least once a week. My mom has always loved Creamsicles and that's basically what an Orange Julius is, in drink form. As an adult, I've found that using local grass-fed milk is a special touch that makes this drink even more of a treat to look forward to. Most recipes are made with frozen orange juice concentrate, but given our abundance of oranges here, this recipe shows you how to make your own from fresh juice. You'll need to make the orange cubes the day before you prepare the drinks.

Juice of 8 navel oranges (2 cups)

¼ cup sugar

2 cups whole milk

½ teaspoon pure vanilla extract

1½ to 2 cups ice

1. Stir together the orange juice and sugar in a small saucepan. Bring to a boil over medium-high heat, then cook it at a low boil, stirring often, until the juice reduces by almost half, about 20 minutes. You should end up with about 1¼ cups of concentrated juice. Remove from the heat and allow to cool for 15 minutes.

2. Pour the juice into an ice cube tray. You should get about nine cubes, depending on the size and type of your tray. Freeze until solid, at least 8 hours.

3. To make the drinks, transfer the frozen cubes to a blender. Pour in the milk, vanilla, and 1 cup of ice. Puree on high speed until blended. Add more ice according to your desired consistency. I like mine on the thicker side, like a shake.

Lemon Pistachio Scones

MAKES 6 SCONES

Several trips to Ireland have made scones my favorite pastry, but my fondness for them started when I worked in a bakery in high school. This version has a base that has become my go-to recipe. It's a cross between the sweet biscuitlike scones we made at that bakery, tender enough to enjoy alone, and the crumbly, drier versions I encounter in Europe, meant to be served with clotted cream and jam. The day I met with Christina Ng (page 132) and Mannah Gbeh (page 134), we got to talk as we walked through the lemon trees on the farm. That day inspired the use of lots of tangy lemon, along with bits of buttery pistachio in one of my favorite recipes.

½ cup sugar

Zest of 2 lemons

3 cups (360 g) all-purpose flour,
    plus more for dusting

1 tablespoon baking powder

½ teaspoon fine sea salt

8 tablespoons (1 stick) cold unsalted butter, cubed

½ cup roasted, salted pistachios

1 cup whole milk, plus more as needed

Glaze and Topping

⅔ cup confectioners' sugar

1 tablespoon fresh lemon juice,
    plus more as needed

Pinch of fine sea salt

2 tablespoons chopped roasted, salted pistachios

1. Preheat the oven to 400°F. Line a baking sheet with parchment paper.

2. Place the sugar in a small bowl, then stir in the lemon zest. Use a fork or clean fingers to press the zest into the sugar to distribute the citrus oils. Set aside.

3. Stir together the flour, baking powder, and salt in a large bowl. Add the butter and use two knives or a pastry blender work the butter into the flour until it is evenly distributed in pea-size pieces. Stir in the lemon sugar and then the pistachios.

4. Slowly stir in the cup of milk and continue to blend until a dough is formed. You want a dough that holds together enough to be rolled and cut, but that isn't too wet. Add more milk 1 teaspoon at a time, as needed, if the dough is too dry to handle.

5. Place the dough ball on a flat surface dusted with flour, and pat and shape to a rectangle that is 6 by 8 inches. Cut in six squares. Place the squares on the prepared baking sheet. Bake for 20 minutes, until the edges are golden brown and centers firm.

6. Remove from the oven and let the scones cool for 30 minutes while you make the glaze.

7. Make the glaze: Stir together the confectioners' sugar and tablespoon of lemon juice in a small bowl. Stir in the salt and continue to stir until a glaze forms that is thick enough to drizzle. If needed, add a little more lemon juice to reach the drizzle consistency.

8. Once the scones have cooled, drizzle each with glaze. Sprinkle the tops with chopped pistachios. You can eat them right away, or let the glaze set and harden a bit if you plan to transport them.

CHEF CHRISTINA NG

PERSONAL CHEF AND FOOD EDUCATOR, SAN DIEGO

I first met Christina in 2020. I had been invited to present at a conference for farmers' market professionals in San Diego and it held an event to promote my book *Beer Bread*. Christina was the one who prepared my recipes from the book to share at that event. I'm not too proud to say that her results were better than mine. I knew right away that she loves what she does and that she is also skilled at it.

Christina is a personal chef who also caters private events. She now lives in San Diego, but she's from the Bay Area. She says, "I grew up in San Francisco and had the fortune to be in a very diverse city and try a lot of different foods."

She began studying food science and quickly learned that she loved the food, but not so much the science. Her place is at the production level, making food to share. "That's the path in food I wanted to take," she says.

Local food is as much about people as it is ingredients, for Christina. "I've gotten to meet some of the most amazing people and some of the most important people in my life at the farmers' market. It goes beyond the food," she says.

In 2019, she began working part time for the Berry Good Food Foundation, an organization that supports a local and regenerative food system in San Diego and Baja California. In her role as Foundation Cultivator, she was able to see the organization through its transition to a focus on healthy, whole foods that are accessible to everyone. Christina operates the school garden grant program and its garden as well as culinary classes.

"I really like where I'm at, not hustling to keep my calendar full of only private chef clients and events. I've been able to give back and create longevity with my work," Christina says.

She's always been driven by the fact that she can touch so many lives with one bite of food. Now, she's found that teaching is even more rewarding than only sharing a food. By teaching others to prepare food, she's providing a memory and experience that has the potential to live on forever.

She describes food as a mantra in the state. "We have a gamut of produce that chefs can work with. I feel extremely lucky that I live in California," she says.

Tangerine Chicken Lettuce Wraps

SERVES 4 TO 6 AS A STARTER

The fresh juices of tangerines and limes give the ground chicken in these self-assembled wraps a punch of sweet citrus. They are easy to make as a simple starter or you can turn them into your meal. I find the delicate flavor and tender leaves of butter lettuce to be the best choice for lettuce wraps because they don't overpower the flavor of the filling.

⅓ cup tangerine juice (from 1 to 2 tangerines)

2 teaspoons fresh lime juice (from ½ lime)

2 teaspoons low-sodium soy sauce

1 teaspoon light brown sugar

½ teaspoon toasted sesame oil

2 teaspoons cornstarch

1 pound ground chicken

3 tablespoons minced yellow onion

2 garlic cloves, grated

4 scallions, sliced, green and white parts separated

½ teaspoon chili crisp or chili crunch

½ teaspoon fine sea salt, or to taste

⅓ cup chopped salted peanuts

1 head butter lettuce, leaves separated and cleaned

Note: I add a small amount of chili crisp or chili crunch to the filling. It's a chili oil with crunchy pieces of garlic and chili bits. There are several varieties on the market and it's easy to find online. I use Momofuku Chili Crunch. I love having it around as a garnish for noodles, rice, and even omelets, but if you'd rather not use the oil, you can substitute ¼ to ½ teaspoon of crushed red pepper flakes or your favorite hot sauce. You can also use regular soy sauce for this recipe, but adjust the addition of sea salt at the end, as needed.

1. Stir together the tangerine juice, lime juice, soy sauce, brown sugar, and sesame oil in a small bowl. Add the cornstarch and stir until smooth. Set aside.

2. Heat a large skillet over medium-high and add the chicken. Cook until it just begins to brown, breaking it into small pieces as it cooks, for about 3 minutes. Add the onion and garlic. Cook until the chicken is cooked completely and no longer pink, 4 to 5 more minutes. Stir in the white parts of the scallions.

3. Lower the heat to low. Give the juice blend a stir in case the liquid has separated. Pour it into the skillet, stir it into the meat and increase the heat to medium. Cook until the sauce is thickened and it coats the chicken, 1 to 2 minutes.

4. Stir in the chili crunch and add the salt, adjusting it to taste.

5. Transfer the chicken to a serving bowl. Sprinkle with a few peanuts and a few of the green slices of scallion. Serve it alongside the prepared lettuce leaves with the rest of the peanuts and the scallions on the side. To assemble, add a spoonful of chicken onto a leaf, then top with peanuts and scallions.

APPLE BLOSSOM FARMS

MANNAH GBEH, BONSALL

Mannah Gbeh grew up in Liberia, West Africa. Agriculture had always been a way of life for him, with his grandfather growing such crops as cassava and rice, but it wasn't until a civil war in his home country sent him to a refugee camp in Ghana that a path for his adult life became clear.

Women had sown seeds into their clothing to bring with them to the camp and Mannah remembers a large event when they all began to pull these seeds out and discuss which foods they could continue to grow in this new place. "That just blew my mind. That was the first time it clicked for me. This is really awesome. This is what you're probably going to be doing for the rest of your life," says Mannah.

It was powerful seeing this passion for food from people who escaped death in their country. Upon leaving, they weren't grabbing material things; they were grabbing seed. "I think the understanding for them was that seed is life. So, for me, ever since then, it's been ingrained in me," he says.

After that time in the refugee camp, he moved to the United States at age 17, graduated from high school, and then served eight years in the US Navy. During his tours in the Middle East, his curiosity for growing food continued. "I came out of a civil war where I saw a lot of death and destruction. I joined the military where I saw a lot of death and destruction. My whole goal after that was to be a farmer because, in farming, you are giving life. I knew right when I got out of the military I was going to go straight into farming," he says.

Today, Mannah uses his extensive knowledge in agriculture and horticulture to operate as farm manager for families and farms around Bonsall

in San Diego County, including Apple Blossom Farms. This 20-acre organic farm grows about 60 different varieties of produce. Avocados, lemons, limes, bananas, sugarcane, pomegranates, mulberries, and kumquats are just a short list of all that the farm produces. While it still sells to some local specialty markets, much of their produce supplies local Community Supported Agriculture (CSA) membership boxes.

Mannah admits that farming is a lot of work. But he's quick to explain that it's not work without huge reward: "It's so amazing to see your kids run around a farm. It's so amazing to see your neighbors when you bring them a basket of food. It's so amazing to see how people interact with food. For me, that's what makes me really, really happy," he says.

Orange Bars

MAKES 9 BARS

These sweet, delicate bars top a buttery crust with an almost jamlike topping that is full of citrus flavor. They make an ideal addition to picnics and potlucks because you can cut them into larger bars as I instruct here, or you can divide them into bite-size bars for more to go around when they are being added to a dessert table.

Crust

1 cup (120 g) all-purpose flour

8 tablespoons (1 stick) unsalted butter, softened, plus more for pan

¼ cup confectioners' sugar

¼ teaspoon pure almond extract

¼ teaspoon fine sea salt

Orange Filling

1 cup sugar

2 teaspoons orange zest

1 tablespoon fresh orange juice

½ teaspoon baking powder

¼ teaspoon fine sea salt

2 large eggs

Confectioners' sugar for serving

Note: Use the juice from a navel or Cara Cara orange here. I know from experience that, while still delicious, the dark pigments of blood orange juice give the bars a funky green color once baked.

1. Preheat the oven to 350°F. Butter an 8-inch square pan.

2. Make the crust: Combine all the crust ingredients in the bowl of a stand mixer fitted with the paddle attachment. Mix on low speed, then gradually increase the speed to medium-high, scraping the

bowl as needed. Mix for 3 minutes. The crust will transform from being crumbly to a dough ball in the center of the bowl.

3. Press the dough evenly into the bottom of the prepared pan to fully reach the sides of the pan. Bake for 20 minutes, until the edges are golden. Remove from the oven.

4. While the crust cools slightly, make the orange filling: Use a fork to stir the sugar and zest together in a medium bowl, working the zest into the sugar so that it absorbs the citrus oils. Add the orange juice, baking powder, and salt and stir well. Stir in the eggs until all the filling ingredients are blended into a smooth liquid. Pour the filling over the crust.

5. Return the pan to the oven. Bake the bars for 25 minutes, until a light brown crust forms on the top and the center doesn't jiggle when you move the pan.

6. Remove from the oven and let cool for 15 minutes, then dust the top with confectioners' sugar. Let cool completely, at least 1 hour. Dust with more confectioners' sugar and cut in nine bars to serve.

McKELLAR RANCH COMPANY

ROBERT McKELLAR, IVANHOE

"My father and mother were very community-minded," says Robert McKellar, who is known as Farmer Bob. "My father was one of the men who started the volunteer fire department in Ivanhoe. They really gave a lot of themselves," he says.

Farmer Bob grew up on the citrus farm that his father started in 1927. After studying animal husbandry and ag journalism at Cal Poly in San Luis Obispo, he moved to Oregon, where he worked in public relations for 50 years. When his father died in 1972, he began managing the farm remotely, with monthly visits back to Ivanhoe. "I was able to do that because I had three absolutely amazing employees. It sounds funny today, but we did everything by fax and telephone," he says.

After his mother passed away in 2002 at the age of 102, Farmer Bob moved back to the family farm full time. The farm grows several varieties of navel oranges as well as Valencia oranges and mandarins. Navels ripen in October, and they are picked at least until May, often until June. Valencia oranges are picked from May until September. "Essentially, we're harvesting citrus year-round," says Farmer Bob.

Their fruit is distributed nationwide, but locally the farm is best known as McKellar Family Farms and Farmer Bob's World, a nonprofit that educates

the community. "The character of this operation is one of giving, which we get from my father and mother. Many of the things that we've done, and are doing, are related to carrying out the beginning traditions of this operation. That's really how we got started," says Farmer Bob.

One day, the farm received a call that someone visiting California from another country wanted to tour, and that is what launched the availability of farm tours. This has led to the many students they have educated through school tours, not to mention guests from as far away as Finland and South Korea. Their wagon and walking tours are for anyone who might be interested in learning more about farming in California and its citrus.

Orange Salad

SERVES 4 TO 6

This will likely be one of the simplest salads you make, and I also guarantee you that it combines ingredients that you wouldn't think of merging on a plate. It's longtime citrus farmer Bob McKellar's recipe. And when he shared it with me, he told me that he doesn't measure it. So the measurements below are from me. I tell you this because you should feel free to exercise your culinary freedom. A couple of extra oranges? More olive oil? An extra shake of pepper? Go for it. Then, enjoy your pleasant surprise as you taste the sweetness of citrus come together with the fresh green flavors of olive oil and the spiciness of black pepper. I find this recipe is best with a small-batch, cold-pressed olive oil that has grassy, spicy notes.

5 medium navel oranges, peeled and chopped
¼ teaspoon freshly ground black pepper, or to taste
1½ tablespoons extra-virgin olive oil

Spread the oranges on a serving plate. Sprinkle with half of the pepper. Drizzle with the olive oil. Then, sprinkle with the rest of the pepper. Enjoy right away.

Bob McKellar, McKellar Ranch

CHAPTER 3

FROM THE PASTURE

I think the most impressive, diverse food category in this state is that which comes from our pastures. Dairy cows and sheep dine on the greenest of grasses in the north of the state from Humboldt to Marin counties. Pastured chickens peck the soils of the Central Valley and clean up postharvested fields outside San Diego. Grass-fed beef cattle roam the ranchlands of the Central Coast, while heritage-breed pigs and dairy goats rest on the tree-covered properties not far from the coastline.

What our meats, milks, butters, and cheeses have in this state is terroir. The diversity of the land used to raise these animals gives us tastes and flavor profiles in the foods produced from them that can't be replicated. The recipes in this chapter use these fine foods along with ingredients from our soils and trees to create hearty main courses, but also appetizers, condiments, and dessert.

Radish Butter with Garlic Scapes and Smoked Sea Salt

MAKES ½ CUP

One of my favorite simple meals is toast with sliced radishes, butter, and sea salt. This recipe is that, minus the bread. It is an easy compound butter that allows for prepping radish toast ahead of time. All you need to do is slice off a piece and spread it over warm bread or melt it over a steaming baked potato. The combination of spicy radish with savory garlic, crunchy sea salt, and sweet butter is unbeatable. I use two kinds of radishes here, Mirabeau, small, elongated red radishes with a white root end, and Green Luobo, a dark green and cream-colored radish with a spicy flavor that Coastal Roots Farm (page 65) introduced me to. You can use any variety you wish. What's essential is that you use a rich butter that is high in butterfat, such as Straus Family Creamery European Style Butter.

⅓ cup shredded radishes

¼ teaspoon fine sea salt

8 tablespoons (1 stick) unsalted
    European-style butter, softened

1 tablespoon minced garlic scapes

½ teaspoon flake smoked sea salt

1. Place the shredded radishes in a colander and sprinkle with the fine sea salt. Let the colander sit in the sink or over a dish towel for 15 to 20 minutes to drip and help pull out excess moisture.

2. Rinse the radishes and then place them on a paper towel. Work over the sink and squeeze the paper towel around them to extract all liquid. Keep squeezing until no more water drips out.

3. Place the radishes in a medium bowl. Add the butter, garlic scapes, and smoked sea salt. Stir just until all the ingredients are evenly distributed within the butter.

4. Place the compound butter on a 12-inch-long piece of wax paper. Wrap one end of the paper over the butter and begin to form it into a log. Roll up the log in the paper and twist each end to seal. Refrigerate until firm, 1 to 2 hours, before serving.

Yogurt-Dressed Cucumbers with Toasted Chickpeas

SERVES 4

Here, cool yogurt dressing with a savory spice blend coats crisp, juicy cucumbers while chickpeas add heartiness and protein, making this an ideal summer lunch. Adobo seasoning, one of my favorite spice blends, is used to flavor the yogurt. It's easy to find at spice stores and online. I find Greek yogurt to be a bit too thick for the ideal consistency of the dressing. A European-style or really anything thinner than Greek yogurt will work well. During testing, it was shared with me that this recipe would also be good with the cucumbers diced finely, transforming it from a light meal or side dish into a dip for pita chips. That idea was just too good not to share, so feel free to exercise your options when making it.

Chickpeas

One 15.5-ounce can chickpeas, rinsed and drained

1 tablespoon extra-virgin olive oil

1 teaspoon salt-free adobo seasoning

¼ teaspoon fine sea salt

⅛ teaspoon smoked paprika

Yogurt Dressing

⅓ cup plain European-style yogurt

Zest of 1 lime

½ teaspoon salt-free adobo seasoning

¼ teaspoon ground coriander

¼ teaspoon fine sea salt

Cucumbers

1 English cucumber

1 tablespoon minced red onion

Cilantro leaves for garnish

Notes: I use a salt-free adobo seasoning. Check the label, and if yours is not salt-free, taste the chickpeas and yogurt before you add the salt stated in the recipe. You may not need it. Also, avoid making the chickpeas too far ahead of time. Once they are stored, they will soften. I most often use my cast-iron skillet to toast chickpeas.

1. Make the chickpeas: Spread them on a clean dish towel to absorb all the moisture from rinsing. Transfer them to a bowl and add the olive oil, adobo seasoning, salt, and smoked paprika. Stir well.

2. Heat a large skillet over medium-high. Add the chickpeas, spread into a single layer. Now, apply what I call the sit-and-shake method. Let the chickpeas sit for 1 full minute in the hot skillet. Then grab the pan by the handle and gently shake it from side to side to stir the chickpeas. Let them sit for another 30 seconds, then shake again. They will sizzle and pop a bit as they cook.

3. Continue this, letting the chickpeas cook for 15 seconds, then shake. Repeat until they are evenly browned and dry enough that they no longer glisten with moisture, about 5 more minutes. Remove from the heat and let cool in the pan while you make the dressing and cucumbers.

4. Make the dressing: Stir together all the dressing ingredients in a small bowl until smooth.

5. Prepare the cucumbers: Slice the cucumber into ½-inch rounds, then cut each piece in half to create half-moons or cut smaller into quarters.

6. Arrange the cucumbers on a serving platter. Spoon the dressing over the cucumbers. Sprinkle with the red onion. Top with the chickpeas and garnish with cilantro before serving.

STEPLADDER RANCH AND CREAMERY

MICHELLE AND JACK RUDOLPH, CAMBRIA

All farms have a sense of tranquility about them, but none like what I experience each time I visit Stepladder. I'm not sure whether it's that the property is perched high in the hills about five miles from the ocean, or it's the harmony of goats grazing near avocado trees with farm dogs who always seem thrilled to see you. I first visited on a tour several years ago, and I've been making excuses to visit as often as possible ever since.

Michelle and Jack Rudolph's farm is well known in the United States and abroad for its goat cheeses. But what those who frequent farmers' markets

throughout the state also know is that it is a fully diversified family farm. The property, an avocado farm, belonged to Jack's grandparents. With a growing interest in hobby cheesemaking, Jack moved from the Bay Area to the family farm to see whether he could make it more profitable. He soon met Michelle, and the ranch and creamery opened in 2015. They now have a group of talented, passionate people helping them manage the farm.

The property overflows with avocado trees, citrus, stone fruits, passion fruit, dragon fruit, and finger limes. There are heritage-breed pigs and beef cattle, and of course, the team of goats that are the source of the creamery's award-winning cheeses.

The day I visited in late January, Jack and Michelle took me foraging for chanterelle mushrooms on their property. We returned to their kitchen to make Pan-Roasted Mushrooms (page 146).

Their love for what they produce and how well they know their land is summed up in their description of the cheese we used and that recipe. "It's tangy, almost lemony, and salty," says Michelle. "It has the herbaceous quality of goat cheese, but it's also balanced by the cow milk so that it's not overpowering," says Jack. It's everything from the mushrooms to the citrus to the cheese and herbs that make this simple recipe so special. "All of it has been grazed in Central Coast terroir," says Michelle.

Pan-Roasted Mushrooms

SERVES 2 TO 4

Although Michelle and Jack Rudolph made this recipe with chanterelles we foraged from their farm,
they encouraged me that it can be re-created with
most types of wild and conventional mushrooms.
The most important part is the dry sauté that sweats
the mushrooms, especially when using wild varieties.
Wild mushrooms get rained on and they require extra
rinsing to clean them, so it's important to let all that
water come out and that those concentrated flavors
are allowed to be absorbed back in. We topped the
finished mound of tender, caramelized mushrooms
with their Cabrillo, a blend of goat and cow milk that
has a lemony tang and earthy saltiness. We also
used their Stepladder Creamery Cultured Butter,
which only deepens the earthy, tangy flavor. Cultured, or fermented, butter is widely available at specialty markets that focus on small-batch, artisanal
foods as well as online.

1 pound clean and sliced chanterelle mushrooms

½ teaspoon kosher salt, plus more to taste

1 tablespoon cultured butter

1 medium shallot, minced

¼ teaspoon minced fresh thyme

¼ teaspoon grated lemon zest

½ teaspoon fresh lemon juice (from ¼ lemon)

Pinch of freshly ground black pepper, or to taste

Grated Stepladder Creamery Cabrillo
    cheese for serving

1. Heat a large cast-iron skillet over high heat. Add
the mushrooms and lower the heat to medium-high.
Sprinkle the mushrooms with the ½ teaspoon of salt
and spread into a single layer. Let the mushrooms
sweat for 10 to 15 minutes. Water will begin to cook
out of the mushrooms so that the pieces are nearly
submerged in liquid. Big bubbles will appear and get
smaller as the water is extracted and reabsorbed. In
the final few minutes, watch the mushrooms closely.
As they soften and begin to brown and the liquid
disappears, lower the heat to low.

2. Stir the mushrooms and move them to the perim-
eter of the pan. Add the butter to the center of the
skillet to melt, then add the shallots and thyme.
Cook until fragrant, about 1 minute. Stir the contents of the skillet and spread the mushrooms into
a single layer. Increase the heat to medium-high
and stir occasionally as the mushrooms turn dark
brown and become completely tender, about 5 more
minutes.

3. Remove from the heat. Stir in the lemon zest
and lemon juice, plus the pepper. Add more salt to
taste. Top with as much grated cheese as desired
and serve.

Stepladder Ranch and Creamery

Goat Cheese Ice Cream Sandwiches with Brown Butter Cookies

MAKES 6 ICE CREAM SANDWICHES

Sweet vanilla meets tangy chèvre and nutty brown butter in these ice cream sandwiches. This recipe takes advantage of high-quality vanilla ice cream and saves time by blending softened goat cheese into the sweet dairy dessert. Then, it's piled between homemade cookies before freezing. The best part is the small bits of tart cheese among the sweetness of the ice cream and cookies. Plan ahead for these. Although they aren't difficult to make, there is a lot of wait time. The butter will need to cool completely, about 2 hours, and the cookie dough will need to rest for an hour. Then, of course, the sandwiches will need to freeze completely after assembling.

Brown Butter Cookies

½ pound (2 sticks) unsalted butter

½ cup confectioners' sugar

½ teaspoon fine sea salt

½ teaspoon pure vanilla extract

2 cups (240 g) all-purpose flour,
    plus more for dusting

Ice Cream Filling

1 quart vanilla ice cream

2 ounces chèvre, at room temperature

½ teaspoon ground cinnamon

Note: Once baked and cooled, these cookies provide a firm base for the ice cream filling. But until then, handle both the dough and freshly baked cookies with care. Roll on a very well-floured surface and no thinner than ¼ inch. Use gentle hands to transfer them to the baking sheet and let them cool for a full 30 minutes before removing them from the baking sheet.

1. Make the cookies: To brown the butter, place the butter in a medium saucepan. Melt over medium heat, gently swirling the pan. Continue to cook, allowing the butter to foam and bubble as you continue to swirl it often, until the butter turns golden and brown specks begin to form on the bottom of the pan, about 3 minutes.

2. Pour the butter into a heatproof bowl, but avoid scraping the bottom or edges of the saucepan. You want the browned butter, not anything that may have burned around the edges. Place the bowl in the refrigerator and chill until the butter solidifies back to the consistency of softened butter, about 2 hours.

3. Place the chilled butter in the bowl of a stand mixer fitted with a paddle attachment. Alternatively, you can use a hand mixer and a large bowl. Add the confectioners' sugar. Mix on medium and then medium-high speed until the ingredients transform from small crumbles to resemble a frosting, about 1 minute. Scrape the sides of the bowl as needed.

4. Mix in the salt and vanilla. Then, begin adding the flour a little at a time. Mix on low speed and then increase the speed to medium-high. The dough will start as small, dry crumbles, then transform into larger crumbles, and will finally come together in the middle of the bowl as a soft cookie dough, about 2 minutes.

5. Divide the dough in two, flatten into disks, wrap in plastic wrap or a similar alternative and refrigerate for 1 hour.

6. Just before the dough is done chilling, preheat the oven to 350°F and line a baking sheet with parchment paper.

7. Dust the countertop well with flour. Roll each disk of dough to ¼- to ½-inch thickness. Use a 3½-inch cookie cutter to cut 12 cookies. You may need to gather scraps and reroll. Discard any extra scraps, or you can form and bake them separately for snacking.

8. Transfer the cookies to the prepared baking sheet. They will seem close together, but they barely spread while baking. Bake for about 17 minutes, until the edges are golden brown and the cookies are firm.

9. Remove them from the oven and let cool for at least 30 minutes before removing from the pan. While the cookies cool, make the ice cream filling: Let the ice cream soften at room temperature until easily scoopable.

10. Place the goat cheese in a large bowl. Stir until smooth. Add the ice cream and stir well. Add the cinnamon and stir until all ingredients are combined. Place the bowl in the freezer to firm the ice cream back to being scoopable, 10 to 15 minutes.

11. To assemble, work one ice cream sandwich at a time. Place a cookie, bottom side up, on a square of plastic wrap large enough to wrap the sandwich. Place a scant ½ cup of ice cream filling on the cookie. Add the top cookie, bottom side down, over the ice cream. Press gently to spread the ice cream to the edges. Wrap the ice cream sandwich and place in the freezer.

12. Continue until all six sandwiches are made. At any point during assembly, you can put the bowl of ice cream back in the freezer for a few minutes if it gets too soft. Be careful not to overfill the cookies. As the ice cream softens, the volume changes. Use just under ½ cup in each to ensure you have enough to fill all six sandwiches.

13. Freeze the sandwiches until firm, at least 1 hour, then serve.

Original Blue Beignets with Honey and Almonds

MAKES ABOUT 20 BEIGNETS

These light pillows of fried dough have tiny pockets of blue cheese inside. The tangy flavor of the tiny bits is mellowed by the sweet honey that's drizzled on before serving. Combine that with the crunchy fried edges and toasted almonds, and they are a party snack that checks all the boxes. This recipe comes from Point Reyes Farmstead Cheese Company (page 151) and gives much deserved attention to their Original Blue, a raw milk cheese that holds a special place in their hearts because this cheese is where it all started for the company.

1 cup whole milk

8 tablespoons (1 stick) unsalted butter

1 cup all-purpose flour

½ teaspoon salt

4 large eggs

4 ounces Point Reyes Original Blue, crumbled, plus more for serving

Peanut or canola oil for frying

¼ cup toasted almonds, finely chopped

Honey for serving

Notes: These are best served warm, but they can be fried a few hours ahead of time. Once fried, place them on a cooling rack set on a sheet pan, then reheat in a 400°F oven and top with the honey, almonds, and extra cheese just before serving. A few edible flowers add a nice touch, too.

1. Heat the milk and butter in a small saucepan over medium until the butter is melted. Add the flour and salt, stirring and cooking for a few minutes, until mixture thickens and pulls away from the sides of pan into a smooth ball. Remove from the heat.

2. Add the eggs, one at a time, stirring quickly, so the eggs don't cook. The batter will be lumpy but will smooth out after a couple of minutes. Alternatively, use a stand mixer fitted with the paddle attachment for this step. Add the Original Blue, stirring to incorporate.

3. Pour the oil into a heavy pot or deep fryer and heat to 350°F. Using a small ice cream scoop, carefully drop scoops of batter into the oil. You can fry several at a time, depending on the size of your pot. Fry until golden brown, turning during cooking, about 3 minutes total.

4. Serve warm, drizzled with honey and topped with almonds and crumbled Original Blue.

Point Reyes Farmstead Cheese Company

POINT REYES FARMSTEAD CHEESE COMPANY

JILL GIACOMINI BASCH, POINT REYES STATION

When I moved to California over 11 years ago, I was introduced to something special: Original Blue, a raw milk blue cheese, sweet and bold with a touch of pepper, balanced by a creaminess that coats the palate. When the cheese first became available back in the summer of 2000, it was California's only classic-style blue cheese.

It was created by Point Reyes Farmstead Cheese Company, a certified Women-Owned Small Business with a workforce that is 55 percent female, owned by Jill Giacomini Basch and her sisters, Lynn Giacomini Stray and Diana Giacomini Hagan. The creamery is the result of these sisters' transitioning the dairy farm their parents bought alongside Tomales Bay in 1959 into an artisan farmstead cheese producer.

The day I visited the farm, I learned that two of the company's top priorities are cow happiness and sustainability. The installation of robotic technology in their dairy parlors helps ensure animal comfort, which includes a walk past the massage brush as the cows exit after milking. The farm is a model for sustainable agriculture harvesting methane-powered renewable energy, maximizing carbon sequestration, and implementing water conservation through reuse and recycling.

Today, that Original Blue is to a dairy and cheesemaker what estate-grown grapes are to a winery. The cheese continues to be made at the Point

Reyes farm using only milk from the Holsteins that reside there. It's also only one of the many cheeses the company now makes. It has expanded its cheesemaking in nearby Petaluma, sourcing milk from local dairies that share its mission and values.

Toma, a creamy, buttery, semihard cheese, has variations studded with herbes de Provence and Italian black truffles from Umbria. Aged Gouda and Point Reyes White Cheddar are other favorites also available.

Jill says, "Our cheeses are unique in style and flavor, but they're also a reflection of the regional high-quality milk that is at the core of our artisanal production. I get asked all the time which is my favorite, but truly that changes every day. It depends on the meal, whom I'm sharing it with, and definitely, what's in my glass!"

Those traveling the state can plan a trip to the Point Reyes location and book tastings at The Fork, its culinary and education venue, as well as set off on foot with guided farm tours.

Deep-Dish Artichoke Bacon Quiche

SERVES 6

Most quiches go wide, resembling pies and tarts, but a deep-dish quiche goes up with an impressive, tall crust. That tall crust is held in place while baking with the help of a springform pan. Then, it's filled with a creamy egg custard layered with bacon, artichokes, and cheese. This recipe takes a bit of time and effort, but it's worth it when the quiche hits the table. You can choose your favorite, shreddable cheese. I often use Point Reyes Farmstead Cheese Company (page 151) Toma or Toma Provence.

Crust

2 cups (240 g) all-purpose flour,
**   plus more for dusting**

4 tablespoons (½ stick) cold unsalted butter, cubed

½ teaspoon fine sea salt

1 large egg

4 to 5 tablespoons cold water

Filling

6 slices bacon, chopped

1 small yellow onion, chopped (about ½ cup)

3 cooked or canned artichoke hearts, chopped

4 large eggs

1¼ cups whole milk

1 teaspoon fine sea salt

¼ teaspoon ground black pepper

4 ounces cheese, shredded (such as
**   white Cheddar or Swiss)**

Notes: You have options when it comes to the artichokes in this quiche. You can use cooked artichoke hearts from Steamed Globe Artichokes (page 152) or these Baby Artichokes (page 21). You can also use well-drained canned artichoke hearts. Ceramic pie weights are nice to have on hand, but you can fill the crust with about 1½ pounds of dried beans or uncooked rice while it blind bakes. This recipe has been made in both new and older springform pans. If your pan is older with a looser spring and you fear it may leak, consider cutting a round piece of parchment for the bottom of the pan to place between the bottom and the ring before clamping the pan together. New pans showed no signs of the custard leaking while baking.

1. Make the crust: Stir together the flour and butter in a medium bowl. Use two knives or a pastry blender to work the butter into pea-size pieces that are evenly distributed in the flour. Stir in the salt and then the egg.

2. Slowly add the cold water a little at a time, stopping at 4 tablespoons. Knead the dough with your hands, then add more water, a teaspoon at a time, until a dough ball forms that is moldable for rolling out. Add more or less water as needed to create a rollable dough for the crust.

3. Place the dough ball on a lightly floured surface and use a rolling pin to roll into a 12-inch circle.

4. Transfer the dough to a 7-inch round springform pan. Arrange the dough in the pan, tucking it evenly against the bottom and the sides, so it is flat on the bottom and extends up the sides to the upper edge of the pan. Prick the bottom gently in several places with a fork.

5. Refrigerate the crust in the pan for 30 minutes. Preheat the oven to 350°F.

6. Set the springform pan on a baking sheet. Place a piece of parchment paper inside the crust and fill it with 1½ pounds of ceramic pie weights, dried beans, or uncooked rice. Bake the crust, on the baking sheet, for 15 minutes.

7. Carefully remove the parchment and weights, being careful not to disturb the sides of the crust. Bake for 5 more minutes, until the crust is no longer raw on the bottom and just begins to turn golden.

8. While the crust bakes, start making the quiche filling: Cook the bacon in a large skillet over medium-high heat. Stir often as the fat renders from the bacon and it browns, 6 to 8 minutes. Lower the heat as needed so the bacon browns and doesn't burn.

9. Turn off the heat and transfer the bacon to a paper towel–lined plate to absorb the grease. When cool enough to touch, wipe or drain the excess grease from the pan, leaving only about a teaspoon to coat the bottom.

10. Return the heat to medium and add the onion. Cook, stirring often, until the onion softens, glistens, and begins to turn golden in color, about 4 minutes. Add the artichokes and cook about 30 seconds just to warm them and blend the flavors. Remove from the heat and set aside.

11. Combine the eggs, milk, salt, and pepper in a blender. Puree on medium-high speed until frothy, about 20 seconds.

12. Spoon the onion and artichokes onto the bottom of the quiche crust and spread evenly. Top with the bacon and then the cheese. Pour the contents of the blender over the top of the cheese to fill the crust to the top, but don't allow it to overflow. The size of the eggs can influence how much filling results, so if you have a tablespoon or so extra, discard it versus overflowing the crust.

13. Bake, on the baking sheet, for 50 minutes, until the top of the quiche is golden brown and the center no longer jiggles when you move the pan.

14. Remove from the oven and let the quiche cool for at least 1 hour before releasing from the pan and slicing to serve. The quiche can be served warm, at room temperature, or chilled.

Savory Steel-Cut Oatmeal with Sausage and Poached Eggs

SERVES 4

If you've never switched up your oatmeal from sweet to savory, you are in for a treat. The oatmeal in this recipe is creamy, slightly chewy, and filled with bits of sausage. You can top it with any style of egg you wish, but I prefer a poached egg held just a little longer in the water so that the yolks are more jammy than runny. A few sprigs of watercress on the side adds a fresh, peppery note that brightens up the whole breakfast.

4 ounces ground pork or turkey sausage

3 scallions, sliced

1 garlic clove, grated

1 cup steel-cut oats

½ teaspoon fine sea salt, or to taste

4 cups water

3 tablespoons grated aged cheese

¼ teaspoon ground black pepper, plus more for serving

4 poached eggs

1 bunch watercress

Notes: If you use a lean sausage and no grease is left in the skillet after browning it, add 2 teaspoons of extra-virgin olive oil to the skillet before cooking the scallions and garlic. Any hard, aged cheese works in this recipe, from an aged goat cheese to aged Gouda.

1. Heat a large, deep skillet over medium-high. I use cast iron. Add the sausage and cook until completely browned and no longer pink, breaking it up into small pieces, 5 to 7 minutes.

2. Turn off the heat and transfer the sausage to a bowl or plate that has been lined with paper towels if there is excess grease. Wipe any excess grease from the skillet, leaving only a thin layer in the bottom of the pan.

3. Return the heat to medium-high. Reserve about 1 tablespoon of the green portion of the scallions for serving. Add the remaining scallions and garlic to the skillet. Cook until glistening and aromatic, about 2 minutes. Stir in the oats and cook for 1 minute. Add ¼ teaspoon of the salt.

4. Lower the heat to medium and add 2 cups of the water. Stir occasionally, increasing the heat slightly so that the oats come to a low boil. Cook until the liquid reduces by about half, 5 minutes, still stirring occasionally.

5. Add the remaining 2 cups of water and bring the oats back to a boil. Adjust the heat as needed to prevent the oats from boiling over. Cook until the oats are tender, 15 more minutes. The liquid will turn from foamy to creamy as it is absorbed into the oats. Stir often, then constantly as the oats approach 15 minutes of cooking, to prevent them from sticking to the bottom of the skillet.

6. Stir in the cooked sausage, cheese, pepper, and remaining ¼ teaspoon of salt, or more if desired.

7. Place one-quarter of the oats on each of four plates. Top each serving with an egg, sprinkle with pepper and a few reserved scallions, and serve with a small handful of watercress alongside.

Garden Deviled Eggs

SERVES 6 TO 8

Whether Thanksgiving dinner or a Father's Day cook-out, my family has never had a gathering without deviled eggs. So, naturally, I consider myself a bit of an expert, having eaten them for roughly 45 years. I'm picky about the ones I make myself. I like the filling to be more smooth egg yolk than mayonnaise, and I enjoy adding bits of flavor. In this recipe, I look to the farmers' market for carrots and fresh herbs to brighten things up. Topping them with edible flowers makes the eggs festive for family celebrations.

6 large eggs, hard boiled

5 tablespoons mayonnaise

2 ounces cream cheese, softened

1 small carrot, shredded and chopped (¼ cup)

1 tablespoon minced fresh chives

1 teaspoon minced fresh tarragon

¼ teaspoon fine sea salt

⅛ teaspoon ground black pepper

Tarragon leaves for garnish

Edible flowers for garnish

1. Peel and halve the hard-boiled eggs. Transfer the yolks to a medium bowl. Arrange the white halves, cut side up, on a platter.

2. Add the mayonnaise and cream cheese to the yolks. Stir well, smashing the yolks and blending the cream cheese and mayonnaise together. Continue to stir until thick but smooth, with no clumps of yolk. Stir in the chives, tarragon, salt, and pepper.

3. Spoon an equal amount of the yolk filling into each egg half. Alternatively, you can transfer the filling to a piping bag and pipe it into the eggs. Refrigerate for up to 24 hours before serving. Once plated to serve, garnish with tarragon leaves and edible flowers.

HEN AND HARVEST FARM

ALEXANDRIA MIRANDA, TURLOCK

"We are a true pasture-raised system. That means animals live on pasture all day, every day and they are consistently rotated," Alexandria Miranda tells me as we walk across the 5½ acres that are home to her regenerative farm, Hen and Harvest.

Alexandria went from idea to farm in three months. Three chickens grew to 400 literally overnight, and today 600 roam the property where they are rotated every other day, keeping both the animals and the soil they graze healthy. Similarly, 6 ducks grew to the 100 that now call the farm home along with their guardian goose.

"My focus is feeding my immediate community," says Alexandria. She sells her chicken and duck eggs at local farmers' markets and to a few local restaurants and specialty markets. The Breakfast Bouquet is Hen and Harvest's innovative way of helping customers use their eggs in the most flavorful ways possible. The bouquets include such ingredients as kale, green onions, thyme, rosemary, and basil grown on the farm. All ingredients are carefully selected due to their pairing well with eggs. "It's the perfect amount

of ingredients you need for the week to make things like frittatas. It's the harvest part of Hen and Harvest," she says.

Alexandria plans to expand the types of animals at the farm as it evolves. "Animal integration is key, especially in the field," she says. Sheep will soon help with biodiversity and provide wool, milk, and meat.

As I walk around the farm with Alexandria, she shows me the spot where there will be an educational garden and the planned area for u-pick that will host berries and tomatoes. Farm-to-table brunches and cooking classes are all within sight. "It's just the beginning," she says.

Duck Egg Salad

SERVES 4

When Alexandria of Hen and Harvest (page 157) asked me whether I'd ever had duck eggs, I wanted to say yes. I'd like to think I'd been adventurous enough to give them a try, but the truth is, they were a new ingredient for me. She described them as richer than chicken eggs, and when she said she enjoyed them hard boiled, I immediately thought of the egg salad I had planned for this book. They made a hearty, and as described, rich, addition to the recipe. This is a no-mayonnaise egg salad. It has just a touch of dressing—enough to hold it all together and add a savory, herb flavor so that you can pile it high on a sandwich. I think it's best served on sourdough with a chilled chardonnay.

6 duck eggs, hard boiled and peeled

¼ cup cornichons or dill pickles, sliced

1 tablespoon finely chopped fresh dill

1 tablespoon finely chopped fresh chives

2 tablespoons sour cream

1 tablespoon heavy whipping cream

1 teaspoon spicy brown mustard

¼ teaspoon celery salt

¼ teaspoon fine sea salt

Note: I hard boil my eggs in an Instant Pot and found that 10 minutes on HIGH with a 5-minute natural pressure release and 5 minutes in an ice-water bath worked perfectly for the size of the duck eggs, giving them fully cooked but creamy yolks.

1. Chop the duck eggs in bite-size pieces and place them in a medium bowl. Add the cornichons, dill, and chives.

2. Stir together the sour cream, heavy cream, mustard, celery salt, and sea salt in a small bowl.

3. Add the dressing to the bowl with the eggs and stir to gently break up the yolks and distribute the dressing throughout. Serve right away or refrigerate for up to 12 hours before serving.

Tamari-Soaked Eggs with Hibiscus Sea Salt

SERVES 8

A 24-hour bath in tamari and rice vinegar while still in their shells gives these eggs a fun marbled look. The savory soak lightly flavors the egg and then they are finished with a floral salt just before serving. I use Big Sur Salts' (page 224) beautiful hibiscus sea salt, but any floral-infused salt you happen to have on hand complements these eggs well.

8 large eggs, hard boiled, unshelled, and cooled

¾ cup tamari

3 tablespoons seasoned rice vinegar

1 tablespoon hibiscus sea salt

1. Carefully tap each egg on the countertop to crack the shell in several places, as if you were going to peel them, but leave them in their shells. Place the eggs in a bowl with a flat bottom, large enough that all the eggs can lay in the bottom of the bowl.

2. Pour the tamari and vinegar over the eggs. It should cover them about three-quarters of the way up, but likely won't submerge them. Cover the bowl with a lid and place them in the refrigerator.

3. Chill the eggs for 24 hours, turning them in the liquid at least four different times as they soak.

4. When ready to serve, peel and rinse the eggs. Cut them in half and sprinkle them with hibiscus salt just before eating.

FOGGY BOTTOMS BOYS

CODY AND THOMAS NICHOLSON STRATTON, FERNDALE

Cody Nicholson Stratton's family emigrated from Denmark in the 1860s. "Our entire Jersey herd is based off the six cows that my great-great-grandfather had. Everything is related back to those six original cows," he says.

Their sixth-generation working organic dairy farm sits in the foggy bottoms of the Eel River Valley on the North Coast of California. Cody runs the farm with his husband, Thomas, and his parents. His grandparents, now retired, still live down the road. His parents expanded the farm to include beef cattle, and when he and Thomas moved back to the farm, they added pastured laying hens for eggs and sheep for fiber and meat production.

"We do grass-fed beef. Humboldt is particularly suited for grass fed. The grass grows year-round," he says. He adds that they also graze their sheep all year with zero supplementation.

The registered name of their herd is Foggy Bottoms Jerseys, and one day shortly after returning to the farm, they were showing animals at the fair. The other dairymen started calling them the Foggy Bottoms Boys and the name stuck. "We started Foggy Bottoms Boys really to tell the story of agriculture, LGTBQ+, and Jewish farmers. That morphed into its own brand and has grown from there. It is the marketing arm of the farm," he says.

It's important to set yourself apart for customer recognition. "There's a lot of regenerative farmers. There's a lot of sustainable farmers. Our brand is very much who we are as people but it's also very unique. There aren't a lot of people marketing the way we market and telling the story we tell," he says.

Cody describes eggs as the gateway to their brand. Once people purchase them at local gro-cery stores, they often take advantage of their delivery service, which includes weekly specials, making what they produce more accessible. "That's another thing that is very important to us. Access to local, affordable protein," he says.

They regularly host events on the farm where they cook with guests, serving their Turkish coffee–rubbed steaks and shakshuka made with their mutton that shows off the vibrant yellow yolk of their pastured eggs. They focus on heavily marbled meats with greater flavor profiles, providing thicker cuts and a wider variety of cuts. This is the only place in Humboldt County where you can buy a Tomahawk steak and they have become well known for them.

In the end, what they do relates back to their mission for providing the highest quality, pastured protein to their customers. "It's about the eating experience," says Cody.

Shakshuka with Beef and Mutton

SERVES 6

Cody of Foggy Bottoms Boys (page 160) told me that this is one of their favorite recipes to modify for guest preferences and serve on the farm when they host events. Sometimes, it's meat-free; sometimes, they add the goat cheese, and others they make it with all three of their specialties from the farm—beef, eggs, and mutton. That's the version I'm sharing here. The flavors are bright with sweet tomatoes and fresh herbs, while the meat and eggs round out a filling, comforting meal. Serve it alongside tender pita bread or fresh baked challah to help you wipe up every last bit of the sauce.

8 ounces ground beef

8 ounces ground mutton

2 green bell peppers, cored and chopped

1 small white onion, chopped

2 garlic cloves, chopped

3 fresh sage leaves, chopped

1 teaspoon paprika

½ teaspoon ground coriander

½ teaspoon ground cumin

1½ teaspoons fine sea salt, or to taste

½ teaspoon ground black pepper, or to taste

Pinch of red pepper flakes

6 medium tomatoes, chopped

1 cup tomato sauce

1 teaspoon sugar

6 large eggs

¼ cup fresh mint, chopped

¼ cup fresh parsley, chopped

½ cup soft chèvre (optional)

Warm pita or sliced challah bread for serving

1. Heat a large cast-iron skillet over medium-high and add the beef and mutton. Cook, stirring often to break it apart, until barely browned but no longer pink, about 5 minutes.

2. Add the bell peppers, onion, and garlic and cook for about 1 minute. Stir in the sage, paprika, coriander, cumin, salt, black pepper, and red pepper flakes. Continue to cook until the vegetables soften, about 5 more minutes.

3. Stir in the tomatoes, tomato sauce, and sugar and simmer until the sauce begins to reduce and thicken, 10 minutes.

4. Create six wells in the thickened sauce with a spoon and crack one egg into each well. Lower the heat to maintain the simmer, cover, and cook until the egg whites set, 8 to 15 minutes, depending on how runny you prefer your yolks.

5. Remove the skillet from the stovetop and garnish with mint and parsley. Top with the crumbled chèvre, if using. Serve hot with pita or challah.

Foggy Bottoms Boys

CHEF RACHEL PONCE

THE FRUNCHROOM, PAIR WITH CHEF RACHEL, PASO ROBLES

The first time I dined with Chef Rachel Ponce, she explained that to create her pairings, she focuses on what is missing from the flavors of a dish. Unlike most pairings that match flavors, her method uses contrast to elevate wine and beer and not distract from them. She accomplishes the task by utilizing the best ingredients that San Luis Obispo County has to offer.

"Food is important to me because of this community in this area. I pride myself in working farm to table. It's not always easy, but I will go out of my way to support these farms and these ingredients," says Rachel.

The local ingredients she uses to create her pairings play a role in the seasonality and freshness of what she makes. "These ingredients elevate the food. I don't have produce that doesn't taste like it should. The flavor is there. I just have to do my little dazzle on top to make it shine," she says.

It's this dazzle that makes her not only part of the food and wine scene in Paso Robles, but a leader in how this region has grown in its food offerings. Through her brand Pair With Chef Rachel, she works with local wineries developing recipes, consults on food and wine pairings, and cooks for wine dinners and charity events.

Coming to California is what started Rachel's culinary career. "Chicago is home. It's family. It means a lot to me. I love that I have my Chicago twist on California cuisine. Having the twist and diversity of Chicago-meets-California is really what gets me excited cooking here," she says.

It's why she and her husband, Eric, a longtime brewer, opened The Frunchroom, named for the Chicago term given to the front room of a house where people gather. The idea was sparked long ago by a trip to Parma, Italy where they were introduced to a butcher-deli with everything you'd want to eat and drink in one spot. It finally became a reality in Paso Robles. Inside there is an in-house butcher; a deli, Pair With, which is a dining experience showcasing Chef Rachel's food, wine, and beer pairings; along with Eric's brewery, Cellar Fermentation.

Each space is a representation of the couple's passion for local food and drink. It all demonstrates Rachel's dream of bringing a little Chicago to the Central Coast while celebrating California ingredients.

Beef and Bacon Cocktail Meatballs in Red Wine Glaze

MAKES 24 MEATBALLS

The cocktail meatballs we made in my family dunked balls of ground beef in a glaze of grape jelly and chili sauce. As I've grown up, so has my appreciation for more complex, creative flavors, so I thought if you can make the party snack with grape jelly, then there must be a way to make a version using red wine. It turns out that there is, and this recipe is it. I suggest choosing a jammy red wine, such as a Central Coast zinfandel. Crushed red pepper flakes can be used instead of Aleppo chile.

Beef and Bacon Meatballs

1 pound 80/20 ground grass-fed beef

3 slices thick-cut bacon, minced

½ cup panko bread crumbs

1 large egg

1 garlic clove, grated

1 teaspoon fine sea salt

½ teaspoon ground black pepper

Red Wine Glaze

1 tablespoon unsalted butter

1 tablespoon minced yellow onion

12 ounces zinfandel

4 ounces beef stock

2 tablespoons light brown sugar

¼ teaspoon fine sea salt

¼ teaspoon ground black pepper

¼ teaspoon crushed Aleppo chile pepper

1 tablespoon water

½ teaspoon cornstarch

Note: If you aren't familiar with wine varietals, an important thing to point out is that the Zinfandel grape is not white Zinfandel. Zinfandel is a red wine often described as jammy with berry, plum, and sometimes black pepper notes. It's a varietal well known in the Paso Robles wine region on the Central Coast near where I live.

1. Preheat the oven to 400°F. Line a baking sheet with parchment paper.

2. Make the meatballs: Combine all the ingredients for the meatballs in a medium bowl. Use clean or gloved hands to knead the ingredients until everything is combined.

3. Use a tablespoon to scoop out the meatballs and roll into balls. They should be about the size of a walnut in its shell. Make 24 meatballs. Place them on the prepared baking sheet.

4. Bake for 15 minutes, until no longer pink in the center. Remove them from the oven. Line a plate or baking sheet with paper towels. Transfer the meatballs to the paper towels and roll them around gently to absorb excess oil. Set aside.

5. Make the glaze: Melt the butter in a large, deep skillet over medium-high heat. Add the onion and cook until fragrant, about 1 minute. Lower the heat to low and carefully add the wine and then the stock. Stir in the brown sugar, salt, black pepper, and Aleppo pepper.

6. Increase the heat to medium and simmer the sauce for 15 minutes. The glaze will reduce slightly, but it likely won't thicken too much.

7. Stir together the water and cornstarch in a small bowl. Pour the slurry into the skillet. Increase the heat as needed so that the sauce bubbles and cooks. Stir it constantly as it thickens enough to coat the meatballs, about 1 more minute.

8. Add the meatballs to the skillet, stirring them gently. Cook for 1 to 2 more minutes until the meatballs are coated in glaze and warmed through. Serve right away.

Interstate Burger

SERVES 4

Chef Rachel began her culinary career in California, but she will always call Chicago home. She merges her past and present beautifully in the recipes she creates. Rachel says, "Taking local California ingredients and adding my Chicago twist, this burger was inspired by the Chicago Italian Beef." You'll find all the parts of that sandwich in this burger using local California meats. To add an even deeper twist that is true to the state, she serves it with red wine au jus for dipping made from wines of Paso Robles, where she and her restaurant now reside. She suggests using a Central Coast Rhône blend for the au jus when making the burger yourself.

1½ pounds ground grass-fed beef

2 tablespoons salt, plus more to taste

1 tablespoon onion powder

1 tablespoon garlic powder

1 tablespoon Worcestershire sauce

2 tablespoons unsalted butter

1 large yellow onion, sliced

1 yellow bell pepper, cored and sliced

1 red bell pepper, cored and sliced

1 tablespoon sugar

1 teaspoon olive oil

¼ cup beef stock

¼ cup red wine

4 slices provolone

4 onion buns

Pickled peppers for serving

Spicy sports peppers for serving

1. Combine the beef, 1 tablespoon of the salt, onion powder, garlic powder, and Worcestershire in a large bowl. Gently mix until incorporated. Divide it into four portions and form into patties. Set aside.

2. Heat a large skillet over medium-high, then add the butter, onion, bell peppers, and the remaining tablespoon of salt. Sauté until the vegetables begin to soften, 5 minutes, and add 1 tablespoon of water. Continue to sauté until the water has evaporated. Once it has evaporated, add the sugar and continue to sauté for another 4 to 5 minutes, until all the vegetables are caramelized and tender.

3. Add the onion mixture to a food processor and pulse until pastelike. Set aside.

4. Heat the olive oil in a large skillet over high, ensuring the oil coats the pan, then add the burger patties. Cook 3 to 5 minutes per side for a burger cooked to medium. Continue to cook a little longer if you prefer a more well-done burger.

5. Flip the patties again and after 3 minutes add the red wine. Place the cheese on top of each patty and cover. Let cook for another minute. Transfer the patties to a plate and tent the plate with foil. Let them rest.

6. While the patties are resting, add the beef stock to the red wine in the same skillet and cook over medium-high heat until reduced, 8 minutes. Taste for salt. (Rachel usually adds another teaspoon.)

7. To assemble, take a bun and smear the onion–pepper paste on the inner side of both the top and bottom buns. Place a burger patty on the bun bottom, add pickled peppers, then add the bun top. Pour the jus in a ramekin to serve on the side for dunking, and plate the sports peppers on the side of the burger.

Chef Rachel Ponce
Owner and chef of Pair With and The Frunchroom

Sweet Orange Beef Satay

MAKES 16 TO 18 SKEWERS

My favorite kind of cookouts are those that gather people around the grill where everyone snacks and bites as soon as things come off the fire while sipping beer, wine, or cocktails. Meat on a stick is well suited to this type of dining and that's why I love satay. This beef satay uses thin strips of flank steak and coats it with a marinade of fresh sweet orange juice and savory soy sauce with garlic. A marinade reduction is brushed on the beef while cooking to give it a caramelized finish. Pass the plate around so everyone can take one and enjoy them hot while mingling in the backyard. Plan ahead and soak your wood skewers in water an hour or so before cooking, so they hold up better on the grill.

1 pound flank steak

1 cup orange juice (from 6 to 7 small oranges)

¼ cup low-sodium soy sauce

¼ cup light brown sugar

1 tablespoon unseasoned rice vinegar

½ teaspoon crushed red pepper flakes

3 garlic cloves, grated

1 tablespoon peanut oil

1 tablespoon sesame seeds

2 teaspoons sesame oil

¼ teaspoon fine sea salt

Toasted sesame seeds for garnish

Cilantro leaves for garnish

Orange slices for serving

1. Use a meat mallet tenderizer to pound the flank steak to a ½-inch thickness. Cut the piece of steak in half with the grain so that you have two pieces of steak that are about 5 inches wide against the grain.

2. Slice against the grain into ½-inch slices. They will get shorter as you work your way to the end. Lay each piece cut side down and use your fingers to flatten and spread the meat to a thin piece that can be skewered.

3. Thread each piece on a wooden skewer that has been soaked in water. Lay them in a 9-by-13-inch baking pan.

4. Combine the orange juice and soy sauce in a medium bowl. Stir in the brown sugar, rice vinegar, and red pepper flakes until the brown sugar is mostly dissolved. This is your marinade. Pour ½ cup of the marinade into a small saucepan and set aside.

5. Add the garlic, peanut oil, sesame seeds, and 1 teaspoon of sesame oil to the bowl with the remaining marinade and stir or whisk to combine.

6. Pour the contents of the bowl over the beef skewers. Move them around to coat each piece. Cover and marinate in the refrigerator for at least 1 hour, flipping them in the marinade at least once.

7. While the meat marinates, bring the contents of the saucepan to a boil. Cook until it reduces by half, 4 to 5 minutes. Transfer to a bowl and stir in the remaining teaspoon of sesame oil and the salt.

8. Heat a grill to 500°F.

9. Place the beef satay on the grill and discard its marinade. Cook for 3 minutes, until seared. Flip and brush each well with the reduced marinade. Cook 3 to 5 more minutes, until the satay reaches your desired doneness.

10. Transfer to a serving plate. Top with sesame seeds and cilantro leaves. Serve with orange slices on the side, for squeezing.

LAZY ARROW AT CAMATTA RANCH

FELICIA AND EMILEE MORRISON, SANTA MARGARITA

Felicia Morrison's beliefs about food come from both sides of her family. "My grandmother is from Indonesia so, growing up, I had a lot of Indonesian cooking and food. I think food needs to be flavorful. It needs to have a spice, a flavor to it," she says. Meanwhile, her grandmother on her father's side was from a farm in Wisconsin. The abundant amounts of food they grew fed their farmworkers. "I always think that food needs to taste good, and it needs to be bountiful. Our children grew up with our house always full of an abundance of food that was healthy for them."

Felicia works with her husband, Mark, and their four children on their cattle ranch in Santa Margarita. The Morrison family has been raising cattle since the late 1800s and is now in their sixth generation. In 1978, the family moved their cattle operation to Camatta Ranch, where Lazy Arrow resides today.

They produce grass-fed beef, Mangalitsa pork, and venison that are sold direct to consumer and through meat share programs. The ranch is also the home of 250 exotic animals, a hobby for Mark, and the focus of many of their tours.

"We work as a team, as a family. Emilee started gathering cattle when she was five," says Felicia. Emilee returned to the farm in 2021 after earning a degree in ag business from Montana State University. She now works with the adventures and gatherings on the ranch to amplify the work they do and give guests the opportunity to experience a Western lifestyle.

Whether visitors come to the ranch for a farm stay or for a gathering, a highlight of the experience is the food. Those staying on the property can pick heirloom fruits and vegetables, and when Felicia prepares the meals for events, she uses everything she can from the farm, including its beef.

"About 75 percent of this ranch is filaree. Filaree is one of the best cattle feeds in all of San Luis Obispo County. The seeds act like grain, so the meat ends up being like grain fed, but it's not. It's grass fed, grass finished," says Felicia.

Their food nourishes people while Lazy Arrow Outdoor Adventures allows others to experience their way of life. "We get a lot of people who come here and say they wish they could do this. They want to have this lifestyle, but they aren't able to," says Felicia. Lazy Arrow's direct sales and meat share club provide consumers with meat the Morrison family has enjoyed for years, while encouraging them to take the opportunity to come to the ranch for events, gatherings, and tours.

Beef Tartare

SERVES 2 TO 4

This recipe shared by Pico Los Alamos (page 180) celebrates our abundance of grass-fed beef in the state. It combines a unique blend of whole grains, herbs, and seeds for a beautifully balanced first course. The recipe uses the bavette steak cut, also known as the sirloin flap or flap steak. It's not difficult to find and seeking it out provides the opportunity to start up a conversation with your local rancher and butcher. Do your best to find chocolate mint, even if you need to buy a new plant at the garden store. It adds a distinctive flavor. If you can't find it, you can substitute standard culinary mint.

3 cups water

1½ ounces rye berries

3 ounces grass-fed bavette steak

1 shallot, shaved paper thin

15 fresh chocolate mint leaves, chopped

1 tablespoon toasted sunflower seeds

2 tablespoons olive oil

1 teaspoon sherry vinegar

Salt and black pepper to taste

1 tablespoon crème fraîche

Small fresh chocolate mint leaves for garnish

1. Place a medium, freezer-safe bowl in the freezer.

2. Bring the water to boil over medium-high heat in a medium pot.

3. While the water comes to a boil, place the rye berries in a dry skillet. Over medium-high heat, toast the rye, tossing it in the pan until you smell the deep toasted aroma, the grains begin to darken slightly, and you hear a few pops, 3 to 4 minutes.

4. Lower the heat of the water to medium and carefully add the roasted rye to the boiling water. Stay close by and lower the heat if the water rises as you add the grains. Boil the rye as you would pasta, until the grains are tender but still have a bit of an al dente texture, 5 to 7 minutes. Drain and discard the water. Transfer the rye to the bowl in the freezer and chill in the freezer while you prepare the other ingredients.

5. Chop the steak into small dice or mince it for even finer pieces, to your preference.

6. Remove the rye from the freezer and stir in the diced steak, shallot, mint, sunflower seeds, olive oil, vinegar, and salt and pepper to taste.

7. Plate for serving and top with crème fraîche to be stirred into the tartare as it's eaten. Garnish with small mint leaves.

Pico Los Alamos

Santa Maria–Style Grilled Ribeye Steak with Fresh Herbs

SERVES 2 TO 3

I've always been grateful that I've had the opportunity to live in different parts of this state, especially when it comes to culinary encounters. Santa Maria–style grills and cooking were something I knew nothing about until we moved to San Luis Obispo (SLO) County, neighbor to the Santa Maria Valley in Santa Barbara County, where it originated. It's a style of barbecuing that involves a grate suspended over a wood fire. It's combining this style of cooking with local grass-fed beef that Lynette Sonne loves most.

Lynette is the founder of FARMstead ED, home of the SLO County Farm Trail, an organization that connects local farms while educating the community about these farms and the local foods at their fingertips. "I love to entertain, to have people over to the house. I grew up with that. And Santa Maria–style barbecue was how meat was cooked most of the time. The thing about this type of cooking is that it's very communal," Lynette says. She made this recipe for me using Lazy Arrow's grass-fed beef at Camatta Ranch and now I'm sharing it here with you. "Rubbing the steak with olive oil is the key to keeping the juices inside the steak as it sears," says Lynette. This recipe is for one 12-ounce rib eye that will feed two or three people, so double or triple the recipe as needed.

One 12-ounce grass-fed ribeye steak

One 2-inch piece green garlic or 1 garlic clove, peeled

2 tablespoons extra-virgin olive oil

1 teaspoon flake sea salt, or to taste

½ teaspoon freshly ground black pepper, plus more to taste

Minced fresh parsley, rosemary, sage, and thyme for serving

Culinary lavender for garnish

Note: Of course, not everyone has a woodfire grill. This steak can be cooked on gas or charcoal. Lynette also shares that it can be cooked in a cast-iron skillet on the stovetop. Sear over high heat, then flip and continue to cook until it reaches your desired doneness.

1. Heat your grill to high heat, 450°F.

2. Rub the garlic generously over all sides of the steak. Then, rub the olive oil over the steak, coating it well. Sprinkle one side of the steak with ½ teaspoon of the salt and ¼ teaspoon of the pepper, flip and add the remaining ½ teaspoon of salt and ¼ teaspoon of pepper.

3. Place the steak on the grill to sear, about 5 minutes. Flip and cook another 3 to 5 minutes for medium. Continue to cook to reach your desired doneness.

4. Transfer to a cutting board and let rest for 5 minutes. Sprinkle with the fresh herbs and add more salt and pepper to taste, if desired. Garnish with lavender on the side, slice, and serve.

Lynette Sonne, FARMstead ED

Sliced Chicken Salad in Curry Dressing

SERVES 4 TO 6

I've had a lot of curry chicken salads, but none quite like the version I encountered at a resort in Mexico. It's not a place you'd expect to find your favorite version of such a dish, but it made me rethink how I make my own. First, there are no raisins, which keeps it from becoming too sweet. Then, it uses thick slices of chicken breast, making it more of a meal you eat on a plate versus a filling for a sandwich. Finally, it's filled with farm-fresh ingredients: summer tomatoes, sour cream from grass-fed cows, and cilantro flowers. It's easy to make with leftover roasted chicken, such as the Citrus Chicken (page 179), or with a prepared rotisserie chicken from your local market.

1¼ pounds roasted chicken breast, sliced

2 small tomatoes, chopped

¼ red onion, thinly sliced

⅓ cup mayonnaise

2 tablespoons sour cream

1 teaspoon fresh lemon juice

¼ cup whole milk or cream

1 tablespoon mild curry powder

¾ teaspoon fine sea salt, or to taste

Cilantro flowers or small fresh basil leaves for garnish

1. Combine the sliced chicken, tomatoes, and red onion in a medium bowl.

2. Stir together the mayonnaise and sour cream in a small bowl. Stir in the lemon juice. Slowly pour in the milk and continue to stir until smooth. Add the curry powder and salt, then stir until the dressing becomes light yellow and the powder is mixed in well.

3. Pour the dressing over the chicken and vegetables. Gently stir to coat everything in the dressing but being careful not to break up the large pieces of chicken.

4. Refrigerate for up to 30 minutes before serving. Garnish with cilantro flowers. If you plan to serve it later, wait to dress the salad until you are within 30 minutes of serving.

Grilled Chicken Tostadas with Avocado and Watermelon Radishes

MAKES 6 TO 8 TOSTADAS

Every time I make a tostada, I tell myself I should do this more often. The crunchy shells are easy to find in the tortilla section at the supermarket, and they are a simple-to-assemble starter or meal for the whole family. In this version, chicken thighs are marinated in yogurt and spices for an hour, giving it just a hint of smoky heat. A simplified guacamole is spread over the tostada before it's topped with chicken, and the addition of watermelon radishes makes this easy meal as appealing to the eyes as it is to the appetite.

Chicken

1¾ pounds boneless, skinless chicken thighs

1 cup whole-milk plain yogurt, any variety

1 teaspoon smoked paprika

1 teaspoon ground cumin

1 teaspoon fine sea salt

½ teaspoon ground black pepper

¼ teaspoon ground cayenne pepper

Tostadas

3 avocados

Juice of 1 lemon (about 2 tablespoons)

2 tablespoons minced white onion

1 tablespoon chopped fresh cilantro

¼ teaspoon garlic powder

¼ teaspoon fine sea salt

6 to 8 tostada shells

2 ounces Cotija, crumbled

1 medium watermelon radish, quartered and sliced

Fresh cilantro for garnish

1. Make the chicken: Place the thighs in a 1-gallon resealable plastic bag. Pour in the yogurt and add the paprika, cumin, salt, black pepper, and cayenne. Seal the bag and massage all the ingredients together until the chicken thighs are coated. Place the bag in the refrigerator for 1 hour. If you prefer not to use plastic bags, you can do this step in a large bowl, using gloved hands to coat the chicken and cover the bowl with a lid.

2. Just before the chicken is done marinating, preheat a grill to 400° to 425°F.

3. Transfer the chicken from the bag to the grill. Discard the bag and any extra marinade. Grill the chicken for 7 minutes, until seared on one side. Flip and grill for 8 to 10 more minutes. Cooking times may vary by the size of the thighs; just make sure all thighs reach an internal temperature of 165°F.

4. While the chicken cooks, start the tostadas: Peel and pit the avocados and place them in a medium bowl. Add the lemon juice and stir well to mash up the avocado. Stir in the onion, cilantro, garlic powder, and salt.

5. Let the chicken rest for a couple of minutes, then chop the cooked chicken in bite-size pieces.

6. To assemble each tostada, spread some guacamole over a tostada shell, then top with chicken, Cotija, radishes, and cilantro leaves. Serve warm.

Citrus Chicken

SERVES 4 TO 6

I tend to be pretty adventurous with cooking, so I can't say I have many recipes that my family tell me they make all the time. Except this one. While visiting my brother's family in Florida several years ago, my sister-in-law told me that she makes my citrus-roasted chicken often. I felt like that was enough of a guarantee that it should have a place in this cookbook. I've adjusted this version to have a larger variety of citrus to celebrate one of our biggest crops in California. It's the absolute best way to prepare a whole roasted pastured chicken, in my opinion, and now I guess in my family's opinion, too. Feel free to use any variety of citrus; even all navel oranges would work. You can also switch up the herbs and use rosemary and thyme.

2 lemons

2 mandarin oranges

2 tangerines

2 Cara Cara oranges

1 navel orange

2 tablespoons light brown sugar

2 garlic cloves, grated

One 4½- to 5-pound whole chicken

1 tablespoon unsalted butter, softened

1 teaspoon fine sea salt

¼ teaspoon ground black pepper

4 fresh dill sprigs

2 bay leaves

Assorted halved citrus, dill, and
    bay leaves for serving

1. Preheat the oven to 425°F.

2. Cut all the citrus fruit in half. Juice 1 lemon, 1 mandarin, 1 tangerine, and the navel orange. You should have about ¾ cup of juice. Stir the brown sugar and garlic into the juice and set aside.

3. Place the chicken, breast side up, on a flat work surface or a plate. Remove any parts that may have come along in the inside and trim any excess skin around the cavity opening.

4. Stir together the butter, salt, and pepper in a small bowl. Rub it over the chicken, covering the breast, legs, and thighs. Stuff the cavity with one-half each of the remaining lemon, mandarin, and tangerine. Then, stuff in the dill and bay leaves. Use kitchen string to tie the legs together.

5. Arrange the remaining halved citrus fruit, including the Cara Cara oranges, cut side up, in a large baking dish or roasting pan. Transfer the chicken to the baking dish and arrange it on top of the citrus fruit. Tuck the wings behind the upper body almost like it's resting with its hands behind its head. Pour the citrus juice into the bottom of the baking dish.

6. Bake for 90 minutes, stopping to baste or brush the bird in the juices about every 15 minutes. Bake until it reaches an internal temperature of 165°F and the skin is dark golden brown. If higher spots on the chicken, such as the legs, begin to brown too quickly during baking, place a piece of tented aluminum foil over the area while it bakes.

7. Let rest for 5 minutes. Arrange cut citrus fruit and herbs on a platter and place the chicken on the platter to serve.

PICO LOS ALAMOS

LUMEN WINES, WILL HENRY, LOS ALAMOS

"One of the greatest things about owning this restaurant and our journey so far has been meeting the farmers, getting to know them well and becoming their friends. And also, fully understanding what goes in to producing what comes to our table," says Will Henry. Will owns the wine brand Lumen, and his wife, Kali Kopley, is a long-time restaurateur with restaurants and wine bars in North Lake Tahoe.

They didn't plan to open a restaurant in Los Alamos. After moving to the area, they were looking to open a tasting room for Lumen. The building became available, and inspired by the food produced in the area and the farms around them, the concept of marrying farm-to-table cuisine with a wine experience became something they couldn't resist.

They opened Pico Los Alamos in 2016. "It's what we like to call upscale comfort food. Top-quality ingredients sourced locally, but not a whole lot of pretension in the way the food is put together and presented," says Will.

Pico sources their meats, produce, grains, beans, and other ingredients from local farms committed to sustainable, regenerative, and humane practices. They make what they serve from scratch, in-house.

Pico's Know Thy Farmer luncheons celebrate their local sourcing and small producers. These events bring a farmer and a vintner to the table to speak about the food and drink before the meal is enjoyed. It's their way of passing on the experience of knowing where your food comes from to their customers.

Will's father was in the wine business for many years, with a passion for representing small pro-

ducers. "That's definitely influenced my philosophy on the restaurant. We try never to order from large distributors where we don't know the source of the food. The wine program at our restaurant is the same way," Will says.

As Pico continues its farm-to-table mission, Will has begun farming his own vineyard. While Lumen has always sourced Santa Barbara–area grapes, they now own 12 acres of vineyards in the Santa Maria Valley. "It's always been my dream to grow from ground to glass and control every aspect of it," he says. Lumen Wines can be experienced in the tasting room just next door to the restaurant.

Fried Chicken Sliders with Hot Apricot Jam

MAKES 12 SLIDERS

With so many innovative farmers and agricultural universities in California, it's not uncommon to find a variety of fruit or vegetable that got its start here. The Fresno chile, created in Fresno County, is a good example. It's a red, fruity chile that falls at a heat level somewhere between a jalapeño and a serrano. I love using it in fruit jams, such as the one that tops these fried chicken sliders. This recipe makes more jam than you'll use on the sandwiches, and that was done on purpose. It's too good not to take full advantage of apricot season and have extra to share with others, to top some cream cheese for crackers, or to spoon over ice cream.

Hot Apricot Jam

12 apricots, pitted and chopped, (about 1½ pounds)

1 cup sugar

⅓ cup water

**2 to 4 Fresno chiles, stems and
     seeds removed, minced**

Sliders

1½ pounds boneless, skinless chicken breasts

1 cup all-purpose flour

1 teaspoon fine sea salt, plus more for seasoning

¼ teaspoon ground black pepper

2 large eggs

1½ cups panko bread crumbs

Oil for frying

12 slider buns or rolls

Mayonnaise

12 small pieces of butter lettuce

Notes: When made with two Fresno chile peppers with their seeds removed, the jam is comfortably warm with some lingering heat. If you want a truly hot jam, mince four peppers or consider leaving in the seeds. If you can't find Fresno chiles, a jalapeño or serrano will work, but I'd opt for a fruitier, although also much hotter, pepper, such as Scotch bonnet or habanero. I use peanut oil for frying, but any of your favorite frying oils, such as vegetable, canola, or corn, will work.

1. Make the jam: Place the apricots, sugar, water, and chiles in a small pot. Stir, then place over medium-high heat. Bring to a boil. While you wait for it to come to a boil, place a small plate in the freezer. You will use this to test whether the jam is done.

2. Boil the jam until it thickens, mashing the apricots as they soften, about 10 minutes. Lower the heat as needed to prevent the jam from burning but still maintain a boil. Stir the jam more often as you approach 10 minutes, as it will begin to stick to the bottom of the pot.

3. Lower the heat to low. Take the plate from the freezer and spoon a small amount of jam onto it. Return it to the freezer for 1 minute. Continue to stir the jam while you wait. Retrieve the plate, tilt it, and run your spoon through the jam. It should be thick and spreadable, not runny. Continue to cook the jam for 1 to 2 more minutes if it is not ready, then test again.

4. Once thickened, remove the jam from the heat. Carefully pour it into a heat-safe bowl or jar. It will make about 2¼ cups. Refrigerate until ready to use. It will stay fresh for about 4 days.

5. Make the sliders: Cut the chicken breasts into ½-inch-thick slices, starting at the largest end. Cut at a slight angle or on the bias through the breast.

continues . . .

Each piece will not be exactly the same size, but aim for 12 similarly sized pieces. Pound thicker pieces with a meat tenderizer to flatten the breast pieces so that all are a similar thickness.

6. Gather three shallow bowls and a plate or tray, to prep the chicken. Stir together the flour, the teaspoon of salt, and the ¼ teaspoon of pepper in one. Crack the eggs into the second and beat gently with a fork until the yolks are blended with the egg whites. Place the panko crumbs in the third.

7. Working one piece at a time, dust the chicken lightly in the seasoned flour, coat with egg, then coat with the panko by turning it over a few times in the crumbs. Place the pieces on the plate or tray.

8. Prepare either a 5-quart Dutch oven or an electric deep fryer and fill it about one-third full with oil. Heat the oil to 375°F. Line a clean plate or tray with paper towels.

9. Working with a few pieces at a time to avoid overcrowding, fry the chicken until dark golden brown and no longer pink, about 5 minutes. The cooking time will vary by the size and thickness of each piece.

10. Transfer the cooked chicken pieces to the prepared plate to absorb any excess oil. Sprinkle generously with fine sea salt.

11. Assemble the sliders: Spread your desired amount of mayonnaise on the bottom half of each bun, top with a piece of lettuce and then the chicken. Spoon on a generous amount of jam as desired and add the bun top. Serve right away.

Date Bacon and Bourbon Jam

MAKES ABOUT 1 CUP

I lived for 10 years in Lexington, Kentucky, and it's where I became a bourbon lover. This recipe is a past-meets-present creation for me. Bourbon from my time in Kentucky merges with sweet dates of California and pastured pork bacon. This decadent jam is sweet, savory, and boozy, so what's not to love? It can be spread on slices of toast or used to top burgers; know that you are in a judgment-free zone should you decide to eat it by the spoonful. Large, ripe dates, such as Medjool, work well. They will mash as you chop them, which only adds to the smooth texture of the jam.

8 ounces bacon, chopped (about 8 slices)

1 garlic clove, minced

1 small shallot, minced

6 large dates, pitted and chopped

¼ teaspoon ground cinnamon

¼ teaspoon ground ginger

¼ teaspoon fine sea salt

¼ teaspoon smoked paprika

3 tablespoons bourbon

1 tablespoon honey

2 tablespoons salted butter

1. Heat a large cast-iron skillet over medium-high. Add the bacon and cook, stirring often, until the fat renders and the bacon turns golden brown, about 8 minutes. It should still be a little chewy, not crisp. Spoon the bacon onto a paper towel–covered plate to absorb any excess oil.

2. Drain and discard all but about 1 teaspoon of the oil covering the bottom of the skillet. Return the skillet to medium heat and add the garlic and shallot. Cook for 1 minute, until aromatic. Stir in the dates, cinnamon, ginger, salt, and paprika. Smash the dates into the other ingredients to form a paste. Cook for about 1 more minute.

3. Remove the pan from the heat. Carefully stir in the bourbon and then the honey.

4. Return the pan to low heat. Stir in the butter until melted, 3 to 5 minutes. Stir in the bacon.

5. Serve right away or refrigerate for up to 4 days.

WINFIELD FARM

BRUCE STEELE, BUELLTON

When Bruce Steele left his longtime career as a fisherman and sea urchin diver in Santa Barbara, he was ready to feel more connected to the people who enjoy the food that he helps source. When he moved to Buellton to start Winfield Farm 20 years ago, he began with growing vegetables, but soon felt the draw to animal husbandry.

"I'm going to be a farmer; I want to farm something exclusive," says Bruce. He shares that to have success and customer connection in farming, you have to find your niche.

That philosophy led him to a breed of pigs that not only produce a pork superior in taste to common supermarket offerings, but the breed makes quite the impression with looks as well. Drive by the pasture quickly and there is a good chance you'll mistake their curly, furry coats for sheep.

Mangalitsa pigs are native to Hungary and made their way to the United States via Washington State in 2006. Their curly coats can vary in color, but Bruce has the largest registered herd of the Swallow Belly Mangalitsa outside of Europe. These pigs have a blackish-brown top coat that blends into beige along their belly.

Mangalitsa pork has a reputation among chefs, and Winfield Farm sells its meat to many restaurants around Santa Barbara County. Often compared to Wagyu beef, the pork is marbled with a soft, creamy lard. It has a rich yet delicate quality that nearly melts in your mouth.

When asked about how the meat differs from other varieties of pork, Bruce says, "It's immediately obvious for everyone. All you need is a sample of it."

Winfield's Mangalitsa pork could not have a better home in the state. It's an offering that comes

from a region overflowing with a diverse selection of local foods. The land supplies a wide variety of vegetables, and those fields sit alongside subtropical growing regions that give us everything from avocados to citrus. The ocean is only a few miles away, offering local fish and seafood.

"It really is a foodie heaven. We have phenomenal opportunity here," says Bruce. "It's nice to see chefs taking advantage of it," he adds.

Farming fills a void for Bruce that was lacking when he was fishing—knowing the customer. Now, he gets to experience the partnership between restaurant and farmer. "As a farmer, these partnerships make you feel like you're part of the community," he says.

Pork Secreto with Caramelized Figs

SERVES 2

The secreto is a special cut of pork that is known for being heavily marbled with fat, with a melt-in-your-mouth quality once cooked. I learned about it from Winfield Farm when Bruce Steele (page 184) shared a cut of it with me from his Mangalitsa pigs. It's seared quickly in a hot skillet, and traditionally secreto is served medium-rare, which is an internal cooking temperature of 145°F for pork. I'll admit I prefer my meat just a touch more done, but don't go beyond a pale pink center to maximize the flavor and texture of this cut. In this recipe, the meat is coated in olive oil and fresh rosemary, then paired with sweet caramelized fresh figs.

1 tablespoon plus 2 teaspoons extra-virgin olive oil

¾ teaspoon fine sea salt

¼ teaspoon ground black pepper

¼ teaspoon minced fresh rosemary

8 ounces pork secreto

½ teaspoon sugar

3 fresh Mission or Brown Turkey figs, halved

Rosemary leaves for garnish (optional)

Flake smoked sea salt for serving (optional)

1. Stir together 1 tablespoon of the olive oil, ½ teaspoon of the salt, the pepper, and the rosemary in a small bowl. Rub the seasoned oil over all sides of the pork.

2. Heat a large skillet over medium-high. Add the pork and cook for 3 to 4 minutes, until seared and browned on the bottom. Flip the meat and cook for 3 to 4 minutes, until cooked to medium-rare. Transfer it to a cutting board and let the pork rest while you cook the figs.

3. Stir together the remaining ¼ teaspoon of salt and the sugar in a small bowl. Sprinkle the cut sides of the figs with the salted sugar. Heat the remaining 2 teaspoons of olive oil in a medium skillet.

4. Add the figs, cut side down, to the skillet. Cook for 2½ to 3 minutes, until the edges are browned and caramelized.

5. Serve the pork alongside the warm figs. Garnish with rosemary leaves and smoked sea salt, if desired. Slice to serve.

Roasted Pork Chops with Red Grapes in Red Wine Gravy

SERVES 4 TO 6

These roasted pork chops are like a welcome letter inviting the autumn season to the table. Grapes roast with the pork to impart a delicate sweetness, and then the juices are thickened into a gravy for serving. I like to use a light-bodied wine, such as Grenache, in the gravy but I could see a smoky Pinot Noir working well, too. The recipe is written for four pork chops, but with all the sides at a holiday meal, it can easily stretch to feed six people.

4 thick-cut, bone-in pork chops (about 2½ pounds)

1 tablespoon fine sea salt

1 teaspoon ground black pepper

1 tablespoon extra-virgin olive oil

1 small yellow onion, diced (½ cup)

2 garlic cloves, minced

½ teaspoon dried ground or rubbed sage

½ cup chicken stock

½ cup red wine

8 ounces red grapes on the stem,
   cut in 6 small bunches

2 tablespoons water

1 tablespoon cornstarch

Small fresh sage leaves for garnish

1. Generously rub the salt and pepper onto each side of the pork chops.

2. Preheat the oven to 400°F.

3. Heat the olive oil in a Dutch oven at least 5 quarts in volume, over medium-high. Brown the pork chops, cooking for 2 to 3 minutes on each side. Transfer them to a plate to rest.

4. Lower the heat to low. Stir in the onion, garlic, and dried sage. Stir constantly as you scrape the cooked bits from the bottom of the pan with a rubber spatula. Cook for 2 to 3 minutes, until the onion softens.

5. Carefully add the chicken stock and wine. Increase the heat to medium and bring the sauce to a simmer. Simmer for 3 minutes to blend the flavors.

6. Turn off the heat and arrange the pork chops in the sauce. Lay the bunches of grapes around and on top of the pork chops. Cover with the lid.

7. Bake for 20 minutes for medium doneness (150° to 155°F).

8. Transfer the pork chops and grapes to a serving platter. Place the Dutch oven, with its pan juices, back on the stovetop over medium-high heat. Stir together the water and cornstarch in a small dish and whisk it into the juices.

9. Continue to whisk as the juices come to a low boil. Let cook for 5 minutes, whisking occasionally, as the juices thicken from a sauce into a gravy.

10. Garnish the pork chops with sage leaves and serve with the gravy on the side.

Noodles with Minced Pork and Mustard Greens

SERVES 4

My first introduction to mustard greens was at a Chinese restaurant, when I had made the decision to branch out and order something new. It taught me that this leafy green was underused in my everyday cooking. Its slight bitterness adds such balance and complexity to stir-fries, and I have especially come to enjoy it with ground pork. I've eaten the pork and greens alone many times, but the combination is even more exciting when served with noodles as I share with you here. Standard spaghetti noodles are an easy standby, but a rice noodle or chow mein are good choices as well.

1 pound ground pork

½ teaspoon fine sea salt

¼ teaspoon ground black pepper

½ medium yellow onion, chopped (½ cup)

3 garlic cloves, grated

½ teaspoon grated fresh ginger

1 bunch mustard greens, finely chopped (about 4 cups)

1 tablespoon low-sodium soy sauce

1 tablespoon unseasoned rice vinegar

1 teaspoon toasted sesame oil

½ teaspoon crushed red pepper flakes, plus more for serving

8 ounces dried spaghetti, cooked according to package directions

1. Heat a large skillet over medium-high. Cook the pork until browned and no longer pink, breaking it into small pieces as it cooks, 8 to 10 minutes. Transfer the pork to a paper towel–covered plate to absorb any excess oil.

2. Once the skillet cools slightly, discard most of the grease, leaving only a glistening sheen in the bottom to cook the vegetables. Return the heat to medium-high and add the onion. Cook until the onion begins to soften and brown, about 3 minutes. Lower the heat to medium; stir in the garlic and then the ginger. Cook for 1 minute.

3. Add the mustard greens and cook until wilted, about 1 minute. Lower the heat to low. Stir in the soy sauce, rice vinegar, sesame oil, and red pepper flakes. Add the pork back to the skillet and cook 1 to 2 minutes, just until all ingredients are heated through.

4. Divide the noodles among four bowls. Add one-quarter of the pork and greens to each bowl and toss gently to mix the ingredients. Serve warm with extra red pepper flakes on the side, if desired.

STRAUS FAMILY CREAMERY

ALBERT STRAUS, PETALUMA

In 1941, Albert Straus's father, Bill, founded their family dairy with 23 Jersey cows. In 1994, Albert converted it to the first organic dairy farm west of the Mississippi River while also founding the first 100 percent organic creamery in the United States. Today, 12 Marin and Sonoma county dairies, including Albert's, supply milk to the creamery.

"The motivation is that we're a community. I grew up with farms that I loved, and I see farms disappearing," says Albert. "What I've tried to do is create an organic farming model that can help sustain our communities, our farms, and the food system," he says.

Straus Family Creamery's focus on sustainability infiltrates every part of the business, extending from financial stability of the farm families producing milk for the creamery to the implementation of carbon-neutral farming practices. Of course, all this results in nourishing customers with high-quality organic dairy products from milk and cream to butter, sour cream, yogurt, and ice cream.

"I feel there is a bigger mission for myself and for the company than it just being a business. It's an instrument to help make change," Albert says.

Part of the creamery's mission is to provide minimally processed organic dairy

products using no additives or stabilizers. Its cream-top milk in glass bottles is gently pasteurized but not homogenized, making it as close to the freshness of the milk produced on farm as you can get in the local supermarket.

A few of its ice cream flavors, such as the caramel swirl and Lemon Cookie, use the creamery's own cream and butter. They also hold the Organic, Super Premium label. "They have a higher butter fat content and less air, so it's a richer experience than most conventional ice cream," Albert says.

If he had to pick a favorite product, ice cream would be it. He says, "One of the reasons I started the creamery is that I went to school at Cal Poly in San Luis Obispo and I was on the dairy products judging team. I won third place in a regional contest in ice cream scoring. It took me a long time to get it started, but I wanted to make my own ice cream."

With a focus on the viability of family farms, commitment to carbon-neutral farming, and efforts to find and use truly household compostable packaging, Straus Family Creamery is a model California farm and creamery that is being replicated around the country and the world.

Green Garden Dip and Dressing

MAKES ABOUT 1¼ CUPS

This herb-filled dressing is inspired by the traditional green goddess dressing, which can be traced back to the Palace Hotel in San Francisco. While the dressing itself was worth hanging onto, the play and movie it was named for are best left in the past. So, my version has a few twists of its own along with a revised, but still fitting, name. The herbs can be loosely packed to measure and there is no need to prechop. It blends into a thick dressing that I like to use as a dip for fresh vegetables. It's also a good match for dressing an egg sandwich or drizzling over avocado toast.

1 cup plain Greek yogurt

¼ cup mayonnaise

½ cup flat-leaf parsley

½ cup watercress

¼ cup fresh tarragon

¼ cup fresh chives

2 garlic cloves, peeled

½ teaspoon anchovy paste

1 tablespoon Champagne vinegar

1 teaspoon fine sea salt

¼ teaspoon ground black pepper

1. Combine the yogurt, mayonnaise, parsley, watercress, tarragon, chives, garlic, and anchovy paste in a blender. Pulse until all the herbs are finely chopped.

2. Add the Champagne vinegar, salt, and pepper. Puree on high speed for 20 seconds, until the dressing is smooth with tiny bits of green and has a pale green hue. Chill for at least 30 minutes before serving. The dressing will thicken slightly as it chills.

Fresh Herb Ranch Dressing

MAKES ABOUT 1 CUP

It turns out that Hidden Valley Ranch is an actual place, and it happens to be near Santa Barbara, California. It's where Steve Henson began perfecting his recipe for what we now know as ranch dressing that he served to guests of his dude ranch. I won't argue that ranch makes the best salads, but I will say that a homemade version outdoes a store-bought bottle. Many homemade ranch dressings use dried herbs, but you'll get much brighter flavors using fresh. I also swap the standard buttermilk for local, pastured sour cream and whole milk, with fresh juice from California lemons. This is thick and creamy, teetering on the edge between a dip and a dressing. It's an equally good fit for dunking your carrot sticks as it is for tossing with crunchy lettuce greens.

½ cup sour cream

⅓ cup mayonnaise

3 tablespoons whole milk

1½ teaspoons fresh lemon juice
(from about 1 lemon)

1 garlic clove, grated

2 teaspoons chopped fresh chives

1½ teaspoons onion powder

1 teaspoon chopped fresh dill

½ teaspoon fine sea salt

⅛ teaspoon ground black pepper

1. Stir together the sour cream, mayonnaise, and milk in a small bowl. Stir in the lemon juice until smooth.

2. Add the garlic, chives, onion powder, dill, salt, and pepper. Stir well. Serve right away or refrigerate and use within 3 days.

CHAPTER 4

FROM THE WATER

One of the best things about California is that, wherever you are, you're never that far from the ocean. From Humboldt County in the north to San Diego County in the south, fish and seafood are pulled from the nearby waters by people who have made their life's work knowing our oceans and implementing sustainable practices. The ingredients from our water go beyond fish and seafood, too. The intense flavor of California sea salt serves to complement our dinners from the sea even further.

California was the first place I ever ate a raw oyster and where I first bought a whole Dungeness crab. Uni (sea urchin), whole rockfish, and halibut cheeks are now ingredients I look for, thanks to so many fish markets, fishermen, and researchers here who help educate consumers on how to make the most of their purchases.

In this chapter, I hope to share the knowledge I've found with you. These recipes will have you heading to the coast with a cooler to shop at one of the many fish markets and farmers' markets sharing the bounty of California's waters.

Cracked Dungeness Crab with Garlic Sea Salt and Aleppo Pepper

SERVES 3 TO 4

Preparing whole Dungeness crabs may look intimidating, but there are some tricks to simplify it. Save the live seafood for others who are more adventurous, and buy cooked crab. Then, let the fish market help you out by cracking and cleaning the crab. This will allow you get to so much more meat in the body that is often hiding behind parts that need to be discarded. This recipe creates a blend of brown butter with fruity Aleppo chile pepper and savory garlic salt that coats the crab in a rich glaze. I use Big Sur Salts' (page 224) Gavilán Garlic Salt here because it's full of intense savory flavors from local garlic, green onion, and mustard flowers. This cooked crab makes a pretty platter, but it's also fun to keep things casual and serve it over paper at the center of the table with extra pepper, salt, and a seafood cracker, along with lemon bowls and lots of napkins for cleanup after the meal.

6 tablespoons (¾ stick) unsalted butter

1 scallion, finely chopped

1 teaspoon crushed Aleppo chile pepper

1 teaspoon garlic salt

3 cooked crabs (about 2 pounds each), cracked and cleaned

Chopped fresh chives for garnish

1. Melt the butter in a large stockpot over medium heat. Just before the butter is fully melted, add the scallion and cook until fragrant, 1 minute. Stir in the Aleppo pepper and garlic salt.

2. Add the crabs and stir to coat all the pieces in the butter. Lower the heat to medium-low and cover with a lid. Let them steam in the pot until they are warmed through, shaking the pot often to move around the crabs and prevent the butter from burning, about 5 minutes.

3. Transfer the crabs to a platter or paper for serving. Drizzle the butter from the bottom of the pot over the crabs and garnish with chopped chives.

Dungeness Crab Sandwiches

SERVES 2

As good as Dungeness crab is on its own, after a steamed crab meal, I want something that makes the next meal using leftovers a little different. A small amount of mayonnaise mixed with tangy lemon juice and lots of dill with just a touch of smoked sea salt does that in this recipe. Those soft, slitted buns for lobster rolls on the East Coast can be hard to come by here, so I've found that making my own with a standard loaf of French bread from the supermarket is a nice substitute. I toast it on all sides under the broiler to add just a little crunch, and lettuce tucked into the sandwiches adds a nice earthiness with the dill that balances the sweetness of the crab.

½ loaf French bread

2 tablespoons mayonnaise

1 tablespoon fresh lemon juice (from ½ lemon)

1 teaspoon chopped fresh dill

¼ teaspoon flake smoked sea salt

8 ounces Dungeness crabmeat

2 lettuce leaves

1. Preheat the oven broiler. Trim the end off the French bread and then cut two pieces, about 3 inches wide each. Cut a slit in the center, stopping halfway through the loaf so the bottom stays intact. Broil the pieces of bread on each side and the top for 1 to 2 minutes, until the bread lightly toasts but doesn't brown.

2. Stir together the mayonnaise and lemon juice in a small bowl until smooth. Stir in the dill and sea salt. Fold in the crab, carefully coating it with the dressing so it doesn't break up too much.

3. Arrange the lettuce in the center of each bun. Fill each of the buns with an equal amount of the crab and serve.

GIOVANNI'S FISH MARKET & GALLEY

GIOVANNI DEGARIMORE, MORRO BAY

"It's a blessing to be right at the ocean, to have all of this," says Giovanni DeGarimore. He gestures to the calm bay beyond the dock and the landmark Morro Rock in view. We're standing in front of a tank of Dungeness crab, and he's explaining to me how filtering water directly from the bay off the Pacific Ocean into these tanks keeps their products as fresh, healthy, and natural as possible.

The son of a commercial fisherman father and a mother in charge of the fish market, the well-known local story is that the day he was born, his father came back from fishing to find a note on the market door that said, "Gone to have a baby. Be back tomorrow." His dad made it just in time to witness his birth, and 50 years later, Giovanni is still at the fish market.

"Local and sustainable are our top two priorities here," says Giovanni. Fresh, local California halibut, rockfish, California king salmon, white seabass, species of tuna, swordfish, shark, and oysters are a few of the foods sourced by area fishermen that are unloaded right onto their docks.

A fish market like Giovanni's bridges the gap between our oceans and our kitchens. The establishment is frequented by locals shopping for a seasonal dinner and visitors who are taking fresh fish and seafood back to their campsite or beach rental. Giovanni's also ships its products. For those who aren't in the mood to cook their own, their restaurant attached to the market serves a full menu of fried fish and seafood, sandwiches, and chowders to enjoy outside with that same view of Morro Rock.

Scrambled Eggs with Dungeness Crab

SERVES 2 TO 3

Over the years, I've had several breakfast dishes that incorporate California's beloved Dungeness crab. It's been tucked into crab cakes for eggs Benedict and layered into an omelet, but none of those options has been as good as simple, soft scrambled eggs with bits of the sweet crabmeat throughout. I add just a touch of tangy aged goat cheese to balance the sweetness of the crab. Any hard goat cheese will do, but I use Stepladder Creamery's (page 144) Goat Milk Cheddar. The most important steps to success here are using farm-fresh eggs, and high-quality butter and milk, along with applying a low and slow scramble.

6 large eggs

¼ cup whole milk

2 tablespoons salted butter

4 ounces Dungeness crabmeat

2 tablespoons grated aged goat cheese

Pinch of fine sea salt

Pinch of ground black pepper

Chopped chives for serving

Note: I like to use salted butter to season the eggs as they cook, then add just a touch of salt to finish at the end. Feel free to use unsalted butter and add more salt to taste before serving.

1. Combine the eggs and milk in the pitcher of a blender. Puree on high speed for about 20 seconds, until frothy.

2. Melt the butter in a medium saucepan over medium heat. Pour in the contents of the blender and begin stirring with a rubber spatula. Lower the heat to medium-low. You want the eggs to cook gen-tly, so you may need to adjust the heat as you go. Stir constantly until some solid pieces of egg begin to form, about 3 minutes. Stir in the crab.

3. Continue to stir until the eggs are cooked but are still surrounded by a creamy custard, about 2 more minutes. Remove from the heat. Stir in the cheese, salt, and pepper.

4. Transfer to serving plates. Garnish with chives and enjoy warm.

Dungeness Crab Salad with Smoky Sour Cream Dressing

SERVES 2 AS A MAIN, 4 AS A STARTER

Our local fish market, Giovanni's (page 200), has taught me a lot about Dungeness crab, including introducing me to merus. Merus is the meat of the leg that's between the crab's shoulder and the second knuckle, and it is quite the delicacy. This thick, juicy piece of crabmeat is ideal for topping salads because, unlike small, shredded pieces that tend to get lost in the lettuces, it holds its own among other ingredients. Here, that merus is combined with a variety of vegetables and buttery bread crumbs that are tossed with a creamy, smoky dressing, making it feel more like a feast than a simple salad.

Bread Crumbs

1 tablespoon unsalted butter

¼ cup panko bread crumbs

¼ teaspoon garlic salt

Smoky Sour Cream Dressing

2 tablespoons mayonnaise

2 tablespoons sour cream

1 tablespoon whole milk

½ teaspoon smoked paprika

¼ teaspoon fine sea salt

1 tablespoon fresh lemon juice (from ½ lemon)

Salad

6 cups mixed lettuce greens, chopped

2 scallions, sliced

½ English cucumber, diced

½ pint cherry or grape tomatoes, sliced

8 ounces Dungeness crab merus (about 12 pieces)

1 avocado, pitted, peeled, and diced

1. Make the bread crumbs: Melt the butter in a small skillet over medium-high heat. Add the bread crumbs and stir constantly until golden brown, 1 to 2 minutes. Remove from the heat and stir in the garlic salt. Set aside to cool.

2. Make the dressing: Stir together the mayonnaise and sour cream in a bowl. Add the milk and stir until smooth. Add the smoked paprika and salt and stir until the dressing becomes light pink. Pour in the lemon juice and stir well until smooth. Set aside.

3. Plate the salad in one big serving bowl or in individual servings. If preparing individual servings, divide the salad greens equally among the plates. Top the lettuce with the scallions and cucumber. Toss gently to mix. Add the tomatoes and crab. Just before serving, add the avocado.

4. Sprinkle the salad with half of the bread crumbs and serve the rest on the side. Drizzle the salad with dressing or serve it on the side for each person to add their own.

Dill Caper Fish Spread

MAKES 2 CUPS

Petrale sole was the first fish I bought at a farm-ers' market upon moving to California. Its delicate, slightly sweet flavor and the way it flakes into fine pieces make it an ideal choice for a fish spread. This recipe provides a way to use up leftover baked or grilled fish, or you can prepare it specifically to make the spread. Simply sprinkle fillets with salt and pepper and bake at 375°F for about 10 minutes, until the fish is white and flakes with a fork. Be sure it's completely cool, preferably chilled, before stirring it into the spread. Serve this alongside your favor-ite crackers. Toasted slices of baguette are a good option as well.

1 pound cooked sole fillets

5 tablespoons sour cream

3 tablespoons mayonnaise

2 tablespoons capers, chopped

2 tablespoons chopped fresh chives

2 tablespoons chopped fresh dill

¼ teaspoon garlic powder

¼ teaspoon fine sea salt, or to taste

Pinch of ground black pepper, or to taste

1. Place the fish fillets in a medium bowl. Use a fork to stir and break up the fish until it is in fine pieces.

2. Add the sour cream, mayonnaise, capers, chives, dill, and garlic powder. Stir to combine. Add the ¼ teaspoon of salt and pepper to taste. You might want to add more or less, depending on whether your fish was seasoned before cooking.

3. Stir well and chill for at least 30 minutes before serving.

THE COOK AND HER FARMER

ROMNEY STEELE AND STEVEN DAY, OAKLAND

"It's not, oh let's be farm to table. It's natural for me. It's just what you do," says Romney Steele. She remembers the days of growing up in Big Sur, being surrounded by local foods. Fishermen brought her grandmother fresh catches, and fruits and vegetables came from the fields and trees nearby.

Seventy-five years ago, her grandparents opened the historic Nepenthe restaurant that is still in Big Sur today. The experience of growing up there has steered her in everything she does. "It was an inevitable goal to open a restaurant," Romney says.

She and her partner, Steven Day, worked farming oysters in Tomales Bay for about a year, and that planted the seed to bring what they experienced there back to Oakland.

While Romney's focus was the restaurant and re-creating that direct relationship with food they experienced during that time, as a teacher, Steven wanted to bring the ideas of conservation back to the youth and incorporate that into their work.

Soon, they opened The Cook and Her Farmer at the historic Swan's Market in Old Oakland, a cafe, oyster bar, and wine bar. To their partnership, Romney brings her expertise in food and Steven brings his community connections and energy. The restaurant is just steps away from the farmers' market that happens there every Friday morning. "We can walk out the door and pick what we want. It's been such a blessing," says Romney. They also work with area farms in West Oakland. "Sourcing from local farms is a more pleasurable experience and you know where your food is coming from," she says.

They highlight local items on their menu with their market salads that use seasonal ingredients from the farmers' market and local farms. Their charred market vegetable is a side dish that rotates based on what's available at the farmers' market.

"Being able to touch the food and connect with farmers is what makes it meaningful for us," says Romney.

Grilled Oysters with Jerk Butter

SERVES 8 TO 10

Romney made these oysters the day I visited The Cook and Her Farmer. The aroma coming from the plate is as inviting as the taste of this jerk-seasoned butter when it mixes into the salinity and warmth of the grilled oyster. You'll find that the butter recipe makes 2 cups, which is enough to top about four dozen oysters. Habanero peppers can be used instead of Scotch bonnet. Remove the seeds if you prefer to tame the heat. Romney notes that the topping is optional, but it adds texture and a finishing touch to the grilled oysters. Asiago can be used instead of dry Jack cheese if you make the topping.

Jerk Butter

2 scallions, white and green parts, chopped

3 garlic cloves, peeled

3 to 4 Scotch bonnet peppers

One 1-inch piece fresh ginger, peeled and grated

1 pound (4 sticks) unsalted butter,
    at room temperature

2 teaspoons molasses

1 teaspoon fresh thyme

½ teaspoon ground allspice

½ teaspoon freshly grated nutmeg

½ teaspoon salt

¼ teaspoon ground white pepper

Topping

⅔ cup fine bread crumbs, preferably homemade

⅓ cup grated dry Jack cheese

4 dozen raw oysters, shucked

Lemon or lime slices for serving

Note: Plan ahead, because the butter will need to chill for at least 1 hour before serving. It can also be made ahead and stored in the refrigerator for up to a week, or frozen for up to a month.

1. Make the jerk butter: Combine the scallions, garlic, peppers, and ginger in a food processor and process until finely chopped. Add the butter, molasses, thyme, allspice, nutmeg, salt, and white pepper. Process until smooth. Transfer to a container with a lid, or roll in wax paper to make a log, and refrigerate for 1 hour before using.

2. Make the topping: Mix together the bread crumbs and Jack cheese in a small bowl and set aside.

3. Spoon a teaspoon or so of jerk butter onto each freshly shucked oyster. Top it with a small amount of the topping mixture and place the oyster over medium-high heat on a grill. Cook until the butter begins to bubble and the edges of the oyster begin to curl, about 2 minutes. Serve hot with a squeeze of fresh lemon or lime.

The Cook and Her Farmer

HOG ISLAND OYSTER CO.

MARSHALL

For wine and land-grown food, the term terroir is given to the sense of place that comes through in the flavor. The fresh waters of the sea have this same impact on oysters, but for food from the water, it's called merroir. This merroir is why there is nothing quite like a California-grown oyster and why Hog Island Oyster Co. is a top producer.

The company began in the early 1980s, founded by marine biologists John Finger and Terry Sawyer. Today, there are over 200 employees farming, shucking, and serving their oysters and clams. In addition to the farm in Marshall, the hatchery and nursery is in Humboldt County and their oyster bars and restaurants can be found in Larkspur, Marshall, Napa, and San Francisco.

"The culinary oysters are a lot of work," says Matt MacKinnon as he shows me a handful of young oysters about the size of a nickel. These oysters were once seeds and are now ready to enter the Tomales Bay to grow to their full size.

I'd never had a fresh oyster until I visited Hog Island's oyster farm in Marshall when I first moved to California, so it's a place and a culinary experience that are unforgettable to me. But the work that goes into putting those fresh salty oysters on my plate is what I learned from Matt, the retail and café manager at the farm.

Farming oysters is a hands-on process. The seeds are monitored daily in the nursery, and once they are ¾ inch in size, they are ready to grow in the bay. The oysters are transferred to reusable mesh bags attached to racks that keep them off the ocean floor. They are placed in intertidal areas, or areas of the shoreline that are influenced by high and low tides. The oysters spend part of their time in water and part exposed to the air.

Oysters remain in these bags from 12 months to 3 years, and during this time, the bags must be flipped. Flipping the racks and shaking the bags is hard work as each holds nearly 1,000 oysters. But the reward is a more beautiful shape and an overall higher-quality culinary oyster.

Once harvested, the oysters are hand sorted for size, condition, and quality. From there, they spend 24 hours in a wet storage system developed by founder Terry Sawyer. The UV-filtered sea water mimics the oyster's natural environment and ensures an exceptionally fresh, clean oyster reaches our tables.

Matt's favorite oyster varies by season, but it's the Hog Island Sweetwater that he prefers to serve at Thanksgiving. The farm grows several varieties that are harvested seasonally throughout the year, while Sweetwaters are grown and harvested year-round.

Shucked Raw Oysters with Hogwash Mignonette

SERVES 2 TO 4

Fresh, shucked raw oysters taste even better with a splash of citrus, herbs, and a little spicy heat. Those are the flavors that come together in Hog Island's Hogwash Mignonette, whose recipe is shared with us here. A splash of this on a raw oyster is one of my first culinary memories in California. Be sure to use both the seasoned and unseasoned rice vinegars, because blending them creates a balance in the acidity, sweetness, and salinity of the topping. The recipe makes a generous bowlful, plenty for a dozen oysters. If you have some left over, the team at Hog Island encourages that it's also good as a Bloody Mary topping.

¼ cup seasoned rice vinegar

¼ cup unseasoned rice vinegar

1 large jalapeño pepper, seeded and minced

1 large shallot, peeled and minced

½ bunch cilantro, finely chopped

Juice of 1 lime (2 tablespoons)

One dozen raw oysters, shucked

1. Combine all the ingredients in a medium bowl.

2. When serving, stir the Hogwash beforehand to include all the goodies in the bowl. Serve in a ramekin or small, shallow bowl, alongside freshly shucked raw oysters. Place a teaspoon near the bowl for guests to spoon the sauce onto their oysters.

3. Use the Hogwash the same day it's made. If making ahead, mix together the jalapeño, shallot, and cilantro in a bowl and store refrigerated in an airtight container. Add the vinegars and lime juice and blend just before serving.

Hog Island Oyster Co.

Grilled Abalone with Hot Lime Butter

SERVES 4 TO 6

Abalone was once a common product offered by California fisheries, and many of the food producers I interviewed for this book have past connections to that industry. Today, it is no longer fished commercially, to protect the species, but we can still enjoy it, thanks to abalone farming on our coasts. It has a firm texture that works well for bite-size pieces, so it's often served in small slices or chopped. During my visit to the Santa Barbara Saturday Fishermen's Market, The Cultured Abalone Farm shared the best way to grill smaller abalone, which is the method I use in this recipe. I like to use a rich European-style butter to hold up to this mollusk, such as Straus Family Creamery's (page 190). It's flavored with hot sauce and tangy lime. Plan for a recipe like this when you want to pass around a snack straight off the grill, because it can cool quickly once cooked.

2 tablespoons unsalted butter

½ teaspoon hot sauce

¼ teaspoon lime zest

½ teaspoon fresh lime juice

Pinch of fine sea salt

4 abalone

Lime wedges for serving

Note: The size of abalone is often categorized by how old they are. Choose medium abalone, about 4 years old, for a grilled recipe like this.

1. Heat a grill to very high heat, at least 500°F.

2. Melt the butter in a small saucepan over medium-high heat, add the hot sauce, lime zest and juice, and salt. Remove from the heat. Alternatively, you can do this in a small, microwave-safe bowl in a microwave. Remove 1 tablespoon and reserve the rest for after cooking.

3. Brush the raw abalone with the tablespoon of the hot lime butter. Place them, shell side down, on the grill and cook for 3 to 6 minutes, until the flesh begins to cup, juices bubble, and the edges darken.

4. Flip and cook for 2 to 3 minutes, until seared with grill marks.

5. Remove from the grill and brush with the reserved hot lime butter. Use a paring knife to separate the meat of the abalone from the waste portion that lines the bottom of the shell. You can scrape the shell and put the meat back in the shell to serve, or slice or dice and serve it on a cutting board with toothpicks. Serve with lime wedges.

Pacific Sand Dabs with Garlic Butter and Smoked Sea Salt

SERVES 4

There is no simpler dinner than a meal of Pacific sand dabs. The fillets are light and flaky and cook in a few minutes. They don't need a lot of fuss, which is why I top them with a simple butter made with fresh garlic and bits of crunchy flake sea salt. Prepare to work quickly and take the fillets straight to the table for serving. Such a delicate fish can cool down fast. Pair them with dressed greens for lunch or serve the Rice and Kale Salad with Herb Vinaigrette and Parmesan (page 42) alongside for dinner.

Garlic Butter

3 tablespoons unsalted butter, softened

1 garlic clove, grated

½ teaspoon of flake smoked sea salt

Sand Dabs

2 tablespoons unsalted butter

1 pound Pacific sand dab fillets (about 8)

Chopped fresh chives for garnish

1. Make the garlic butter: Stir together all the ingredients in a small bowl. Set aside.

2. Make the sand dabs: Melt the butter for the fish in a large skillet over medium-high heat. Work in batches, if necessary, so you don't overcrowd the pan. Add the fillets to the skillet and cook until the edges begin to turn from opaque to white, about 90 seconds. Flip the fillets and cook for another 60 to 90 seconds, until the fish cooks through and the edges begin to curl up a bit. Top with the garlic butter while they are still in the skillet.

3. You can serve them from skillet (add back any cooked in batches before serving) or transfer them to a serving platter. Garnish with chives.

California Uni Toast

SERVES 2 TO 4

Uni, the creamy, yellow, edible portion of the sea urchin, is well known in California, specifically the uni that comes from Santa Barbara. Stop by the Fishermen's Market there on a Saturday morning and you can buy fresh sea urchin cut right in front of you, served open for you to eat as you stroll. The day I visited I bought several and I packed them on ice and made the 2-hour drive home to start creating some recipes, such as this toast. Uni toast has several variations, but this book needed a true California version for the Santa Barbara delicacy, and this is it—a dish that celebrates the state from trees to the soil, to the sea.

1 green garlic stalk

6 tablespoons peanut oil

⅛ teaspoon smoked flake sea salt

⅛ teaspoon ground black pepper

2 tablespoons finely chopped raw walnuts, toasted

4 pieces uni (from 1 sea urchin)

Four 2-by-3-inch rectangles toasted sourdough bread

1. Cut about 3 inches from the center of the stalk of green garlic. You want the creamy, green portion above the root and below the dark green top. Cut in half lengthwise, then slice. Separate the pieces (like you would a leek) and drop them into a small bowl of water to remove any dirt. Drain and dry on a clean dish towel.

2. Heat the oil in a small saucepan over high. It's ready when you drop in a small piece of the green garlic and it sizzles immediately. Add all the green garlic and fry for 90 seconds. Stir to prevent it from burning. It's ready when most of the pieces are dark brown and crisp. Remove with a slotted spoon and place on a paper towel to drain any excess oil.

3. Crumble the flake salt with your fingers. Stir the salt and pepper into the walnuts.

4. Place one piece of uni on each rectangle of toast. Sprinkle with the seasoned walnuts and then with the fried green garlic. Serve right away.

COMMERCIAL FISHERMEN OF SANTA BARBARA AND GET HOOKED SEAFOOD

KIM SELKOE, SANTA BARBARA

"I actually grew up not liking the taste of seafood because we never got the fresh stuff at home. I cannot believe that I am now a fishmonger. It's just bizarre," says Kim Selkoe, executive director of the Commercial Fishermen of Santa Barbara, and cofounder of Get Hooked Seafood.

Kim earned a PhD in marine biology, and her work led to friends often asking her for sustainable seafood recommendations or whether it was okay if they ate fish. "As a hobby, I decided to learn all about sustainable seafood so I would be able to answer them and inform people," she says.

She started consulting for local chefs and then partnered with the Santa Barbara Museum of Natural History Sea Center to formalize the program into a restaurant certification program. During this time, she was approached by the local fishing association, inquiring whether she was promoting local fish and seafood. "I quickly realized that all our fisheries are managed sustainably. California has one of the highest standards for the regulation of their fisheries and sustainability," she says.

"As a marine biologist, I realized I could be of help to the local fishing community by promoting the fact that they're really sustainable. They weren't getting enough credit," she says. Through her work with the Commercial Fishermen of Santa Barbara, they have revitalized the Saturday Fishermen's Market, which allows consumers to buy fish and seafood caught locally in the Santa

Barbara Harbor directly from local commercial fishermen. They've been awarded grants that have allowed them to add a fillet station. "We knew there would be a lot more people coming down here if they could get their fish filleted. And that's been the case," says Kim.

In 2019, she cofounded Get Hooked Seafood with the help of a USDA Local Food Promotion Program grant. "It was really a passion project to bring the Saturday market to people who can't come down and who don't have the skill set to know how to pick out whole fish," she says.

It operates as a membership program, like a CSA, delivering seafood to Santa Barbara, Los Angeles, and Ventura counties. "You tell us what you don't like and then we go out and work with different fishermen every week, small sustainable fisheries, and bring in their catch," she says. They also supply recipes, bios on the fishermen, and information about the species.

"People rave about the service. It's so hard for people to access local seafood if they're not right next to the harbor and people don't know what to get or they don't understand sustainability," she says.

Kim rarely has time for her marine biology activities these days, but she doesn't mind too much. "It's so fun and rewarding to work with the fishing community. It's such a tight-knit community. I'm really grateful that I've stepped up to do this," she says.

Uni Crisp Rice

SERVES 2 TO 4

This is essentially a fried rice, but it's cooked in a way that creates a crisp crust along the bottom. It's a simple recipe so that you don't lose sight of the uni, which is blended in during cooking and used to top each serving. The butter browns as it cooks, adding a nuttiness to the other ingredients. The cooked bits of uni and carrot add sweetness that balances the savory flavors of the rice, while the uni on top creates a creaminess that complements the crunchy fried grains. Medium-grain rice works well here, such as Koda Farm's (page 43) Kokuho Rose. Leftover cooked rice that has been chilled for a few hours is always the best choice.

2 tablespoons unsalted butter

½ cup diced rainbow carrots

2 garlic cloves, grated

2 cups cooked medium-grain rice

6 pieces uni (from 1 to 2 sea urchins)

1 teaspoon soy sauce

Toasted sesame oil for serving

Flake sea salt

Chopped fresh chives for garnish

Note: If you are in a rush, without leftover rice, cook 1 cup of rice to yield about 2 cups, spread it on a small baking sheet, cover it with a damp towel, and refrigerate for at least 1 hour.

1. Heat the butter in a large skillet over medium-high until very hot, about 90 seconds. It should begin to foam a bit and brown. Add the carrots and lower the heat slightly to keep the butter from burning. The carrots will fry more than sauté in the butter. Stir constantly for 3 minutes, until the carrots are browned on the edges and tender.

2. Stir in the garlic, then the rice, two pieces of uni, and the soy sauce. Stir to break up the chilled rice and the uni while mixing together the ingredients in the skillet, about 1 minute.

3. Increase the heat to medium-high and press the rice into a single layer, giving it as much contact with the bottom of the skillet as possible. Let it cook for 2 to 3 minutes, until the bottom is golden to dark brown and crisp, checking it occasionally by using a spatula to turn up the edge so it doesn't burn.

4. Once crisp, turn off the heat and use a spatula to transfer the rice, in two or three batches, to a serving plate. Flip the rice so the crunchy side is up.

5. Top with the remaining four pieces of uni. Drizzle with sesame oil, sprinkle with sea salt, and top with chopped chives before serving warm.

Pacific Red Snapper Tacos with Fresh Pepper Salsa

SERVES 4

Pacific red snapper is also known as rockfish. It's a hearty fish that flakes off in big meaty chunks, making it a good choice for fish tacos. Here, I coat a large fillet in a spice rub and broil it until flaky. The tacos are topped with a fresh salsa made with two of my favorite peppers, the mild Anaheim and the mild-to-medium Pasilla. The seeds are removed, so don't worry about any heat. The fruity, fresh pepper flavor of the salsa and the savory spice rub on the fish go well with a dollop of sour cream before serving.

Pepper Salsa

1 Anaheim pepper, seeds and ribs removed, diced

1 Pasilla pepper, seeds and ribs removed, diced

5 grape tomatoes, chopped

4 scallions, sliced

1 tablespoon chopped fresh cilantro

Juice of 2 limes (2 to 3 tablespoons)

¾ teaspoon fine sea salt

½ teaspoon sugar

Red Snapper Tacos

12 ounces Pacific red snapper fillet

Olive oil for pan (optional)

1 teaspoon ground California chile powder

½ teaspoon ground coriander

½ teaspoon ground cumin

½ teaspoon onion powder

½ teaspoon fine sea salt

¼ teaspoon ground black pepper

1 tablespoon extra-virgin olive oil

8 corn tortillas, warmed

Sour cream for serving

Fresh cilantro leaves for serving

Note: I specify California chile powder here, but you can substitute your favorite variety and heat level.

1. Make the salsa: Stir together the Anaheim and Pasilla peppers, tomatoes, scallions, and cilantro in a medium bowl. Add the lime juice, salt, and sugar and stir well. Cover and refrigerate until ready to serve.

2. Make the red snapper tacos: Move your oven rack to the top third of the oven. Preheat the broiler to 500°F.

3. Place the fish on a sheet pan that has been oiled with olive oil or lined with parchment paper. I like to use parchment, but it does blacken under the broiler.

4. Stir together the chile powder, coriander, cumin, onion powder, salt, and black pepper in a small bowl. Add the extra-virgin olive oil and stir to form a paste. Rub the paste all over the top of the fish fillet.

5. Broil the fish for 6 to 8 minutes, until the rub bubbles and darkens and the fish turns from opaque to white and can be flaked into large pieces.

6. To assemble each taco, top a warmed tortilla with a few chunks of fish, then a spoonful of the pepper salsa. Finish with a dollop of sour cream and cilantro leaves.

FISHFUL FUTURE

SARAH MESNICK, LA JOLLA

Sarah Mesnick grew up in San Francisco and her mother worked around the corner from Chez Panisse, allowing her to see the positive impacts of Alice Waters firsthand. "I watched how this single woman changed the way people ate. Not just in the Bay Area. It spread. I realized that hadn't really been done with fish, and San Diego had all the right ingredients," she says.

Sarah Mesnick, PhD, is an ecologist and science liaison for the National Oceanic and Atmospheric Administration (NOAA) Southwest Fisheries Science Center. The ingredients she speaks of are not only the fish and seafood that come from our oceans, but the people involved in all aspects of bringing it to the plate. "The fishing industry and scientists have a long history of solving problems together here in San Diego," says Sarah.

The one ingredient often missing, though, are people at the intersection where what was once a fish in the water is now food on our plates, the chefs. "It's important to get the value of all these people who think about food together," says Sarah. That's how Fishful Future came to be. "It formalized the alliance we had between chefs, fishermen, and scientists."

The grant-funded program supports regional fishing communities and working waterfronts by moving toward zero waste in the seafood industry through fostering culinary and nonculinary solutions. Their vision is that cultural seafood knowledge is shared across diverse communities while home chefs gain skills in utilizing the entire fish and entrepreneurs transform inedible parts into usable products.

The first phase of the program began with educating on underutilized, what they call underloved, species and getting people to eat what might be unfamiliar. The second phase focused on no waste and educating people how to use the whole fish. Depending on the species and size of the fishing operation, 30 to 70 percent of every fish is thrown out. Education was centered on cooking a whole fish as well as the different parts, such as fish collars, and increasing the number of meals from one fish by using heads to make broth. The next phase will focus on accessibility and finding innovative ways to get fish to people through more fish markets and possible delivery.

"I like to be able to say that you can eat your way out of problems," says Sarah. Her work has often been focused on endangered species, and she's asked what one can do to protect those species impacted by fishing. "Eat sustainable seafood, support sustainably sourced products. Know the fishermen. Support people doing the right thing and that will spread. That's culinary conservation," she says.

Programs like Fishful Future help spread what the word *sustainable* truly means for fish and seafood. It means more than a species that is not overfished or one fished using environmentally sound practices. "We need to expand the word *sustainable* to be the whole process that the fish takes. That there is little waste. Sustainable also means not just for a small group of people who can afford $30 fillets, but accessible to everybody. That's the sustainable future that we want from our oceans," says Sarah.

Stuffed Rockfish with Kumquats, Garlic, and Basil

SERVES 2

I find rockfish to be an excellent fish to grill whole because it has large bones. When you are picking the light, flaky fish from the frame, you aren't fighting to avoid lots of tiny, thin bones as you eat. What's stuffed inside this fish is meant to be enjoyed with this meal. Eat slices of tender, tangy kumquat and bits of basil with the fish. The cloves can be rubbed over the fish as you work your way through your meal. Ask your fishmonger to do the gilling, gutting, and scaling so you can take the fish home ready to stuff. This recipe is for one fish, which I find serves two people. You can multiply it as needed to feed the table. If your fish doesn't want to hold the stuffing for grilling, wrap it with some kitchen string to secure it while it cooks.

1 rockfish (about 2 pounds) gilled, gutted, and scaled

1 tablespoon extra-virgin olive oil

½ teaspoon fine sea salt

¼ teaspoon ground black pepper

6 kumquats, sliced

6 garlic cloves, smashed and peeled

5 large leaves fresh basil

1. Preheat a grill to 425°F.

2. Lay the fish on a baking sheet and rub the outside and internal cavity with the olive oil. Sprinkle it inside and out with the salt and pepper.

3. Stuff the inside of the fish with the kumquats, garlic, and basil leaves. Wrap it in two places with kitchen string, if needed, to hold in the stuffing.

4. Place the fish on the grill and close the lid. Let cook for 5 minutes, until seared. The fish should lift off the grill when you begin to flip it. Use tongs to help hold in the stuffing as you flip the fish. Close the lid and continue to cook for 7 to 10 minutes, until the flesh has turned from opaque to white and the fish flakes when scraped with fork. Serve right away.

BIG SUR SALTS

CARLO OVERHULSER, BIG SUR

"I didn't have any intention of producing salt until the moment I was hit by that wave," says Carlo Overhulser, founder of Big Sur Salts. "I was about 35 to 45 feet up on the cliff and it nailed me. I was soaked." In the process of gathering his belongings to head home, he had collected some of the water in a beer bottle he'd been holding. He found that bottle again in his yard 10 months later.

There was something solid white in the bottle that fell out into his hand. "For some weird reason, I put it in my mouth," he says with a laugh. It was the best salt he had ever tasted.

That event led to the creation of Big Sur Salts, hand-harvested sea salts blended with local ingredients. This salt is special because of three important factors—clean water, minerality, and Carlo's local partners.

"Big Sur has cleaner water because it is farther from a municipality," he says. Additionally, kelp

forests and mollusks serve as natural cleansers, and it's then filtered nine times, resulting in the cleanest source of water possible for harvesting salt.

Minerality is what gives each salt its unique flavor profile, and Big Sur Salts are rich in calcium, potassium, and manganese in addition to the sodium they provide. "You don't have to use so much," Carlo says about their intense flavor.

Carlo is close to the Salinas Valley, known as the "Salad Bowl of the World" due to its farms growing everything from leafy greens to garlic. "All ingredients that go into the salts are from within a 300-mile radius of Big Sur. That's non-negotiable," Carlo says. He works with farms, wineries, and breweries to create his salts. "It wouldn't be the same product without all these partners," he says.

The garlic salt, Gavilán, is made with two textures of local garlic, green onions, and wild mustard flowers from Big Sur. It prompts fans across the country to send him letters. "I have three of them hanging on my refrigerator," he says. Each provides a heartwarming thank-you telling him that it is the best garlic salt they have ever had. High praise from trained chefs to home cooks is common not only for this salt, but the many other flavors available.

Halibut Cheeks with Roasted Red Peppers and Crème Fraîche

SERVES 4 TO 8

The day I met with Kim Selkoe (page 216) in Santa Barbara, we discussed lesser-known cuts of fish and she told me all about halibut cheeks. These delicate cuts are sometimes compared to scallops. They need only to be seared so they are ready to serve within minutes. The cheeks are unforgettable with a little salt and black pepper, but a few things added, such as roasted red peppers and tangy crème fraîche, complement their sweetness and transforms them into a simple bite for a first course or a tapas-style meal.

1 pound halibut cheeks (8 pieces total)

Fine sea salt

Ground black pepper

1 tablespoon unsalted butter

1 tablespoon extra-virgin olive oil

3 tablespoons crème fraîche

3 scallions, finely chopped

3 tablespoons roasted red peppers, diced

Note: The size of halibut cheeks can vary greatly according to the size of the fish. This recipe is for small cheeks, about 3 inches long. If yours are larger, simply cut them into smaller pieces. The recipe will serve four if each person has two, or eight if you serve only one to each person.

1. Sprinkle each side of the halibut cheeks generously with salt and black pepper.

2. Combine the butter and olive oil in a large skillet over medium-high heat. Once the butter is melted, add the halibut cheeks and cook for 3 minutes, until the bottom side is seared and golden, and the edges turn from opaque to white.

3. Flip the cheeks and cook for 3 more minutes. Small cheeks may take even less time. The fish should be just cooked through so that it flakes but is tender.

4. Transfer to a serving plate. Place a small dollop of crème fraîche on each, then top with a few scallions and diced roasted red peppers. Serve right away.

CHAPTER 5

AT THE TABLE

I don't feel that this book would be complete without sharing how to bring these recipes celebrating California to your own table. Both organized and casual weekend brunches and evening dinner parties are a mainstay throughout this state. Whether these events are enjoyed outdoors year-round in the temperate areas of California or pulled together at a long table in the dining room, they give us the opportunity to highlight local ingredients as well as celebrate those things that help bring beauty to the table.

California is a top producer of cut flowers with many artisan floral designers creating gorgeous arrangements with seasonal flowers and natural elements. Craft distillers use local ingredients to create spirits for predinner cocktails. Microgreen and edible flower growers help us bring a beautiful touch to the plate that also adds flavor and nutrition.

If you'd like to pull the recipes from this book into your own California farm table event, these are a few of my suggestions for doing so.

Weekend Brunch

SERVES 6

The following are four recipes ideal for a self-serve outdoor brunch buffet. Each recipe makes enough to serve about six people, except for the citrus salad. You'll need to double that, which is simple to do.

Garden Deviled Eggs (page 156)
Sliced Chicken Salad in Curry Dressing (page 174)
Lemon Pistachio Scones (page 131)
Candied Walnut, Citrus, and Fennel Salad, doubled
    (page 128)

SUGGESTED BEVERAGES

Moonstone Cellars, Cambria—Livermore Valley
    Selenite
Hemly Cider, Courtland—Brut Pear Cider

FLEURIE FLOWER STUDIO

LAURIE GARZA, REEDLEY

"I arrange intuitively. I just do it and it works. And I know I'm really fortunate to work like that," says Laurie Garza, owner of Fleurie Flower Studio. It's why her arrangements are so striking. Her priorities when creating her work are seasonality, and well, you. "I like to get a little bit of knowledge about a person and then make my arrangements according to that," she says.

"Horticulture was my destiny. My grandmother and mom were very much into flowers. I remember everything about my grandmother's garden when I was little," she says. It's what encouraged her to study horticulture, work in nurseries, and eventually start her own business in 2010.

After working as a wedding florist for many years, she began to transition to more seasonal growing in 2016 and then moved herself away from the wedding business a few years later. "I've always grown flowers, but I just got more precise in what I grow and what I want to use in the arrangements I make."

The most important thing she changed over recent years is the seasonality of her work. Before, she would order whatever a client wanted. "I tried for California grown, but I'd order from wholesale companies when the flowers weren't available here. In the last five years, I really started moving toward only California grown and telling people if those flowers are out of season, I can't get them. That is really important to me," she says.

Her niche market has always been those who enjoy a more casual look. "I grow what I like, I don't grow a lot of traditional flowers. Because of my background in horticulture, I've always liked the weird stuff," she says. Laurie loves growing what she uses in her arrangements and starting

her flowers from seed. Pansies and violas are her absolute favorite. Snapdragons, tulips, anemones, and ranunculus are other seasonal varieties she enjoys growing. She's also known for using more original greenery, such as mint in late spring.

While she works within client color preferences based on what is available for the season, she does have favorite color palettes. "I love the spring colors, the creamy colors. If you say them, it doesn't sound like they go together, but if you see them, they do. Blues, purples, pinks, and I love peach colors. That makes it into a lot of my designs," she says.

Customers can order from her website, and she still works as a full-service florist, minus weddings and large events. "I love small events and celebrations of life," she says.

GOOD WITCH FARM

JANE DARRAH, LOMPOC

When it comes to healing both mind and body, Jane Darrah of Good Witch Farm is an expert with firsthand experience. Over six years ago, her microgreen and edible flower farm began with a personal mission to heal herself.

Jane's background in education is social work with a focus on mental health and addiction, which led to her work on a 24-hour crisis response team. Serving this important role in her community prompted her to begin working through her own traumas with therapy while pushing through long days at work and nights going to school. While she was healing mentally, all of this took a physical toll, which resulted in an immune system crash that kept her in bed for six months without a solid diagnosis or solution from medical professionals. The experience encouraged her to return to her interests in organic foods and growing her own foods. A move that both healed her physically and created a new career path.

"I started looking up longevity foods and came across microgreens. I had never heard of them and there weren't any locally for sale. I couldn't find them anywhere," she says. Growing microgreens for herself along with experimenting with edible flowers evolved into a business that prompted her to leave her day job.

She loaded up her product and went from

restaurant to restaurant, sharing what she was now growing. "I hustled it straight on the street," she says, laughing. That personal connection paid off. Her first customer was a nearby Michelin-rated restaurant and today she sells to restaurants, chefs, and in some retail locations throughout Santa Barbara and San Luis Obispo counties.

Unlike many microgreens grown in dark warehouses using artificial light, her products are greenhouse grown in soil that she reuses, thanks to implementing vermiculture (worm composting), which creates a sustainable operation. Her methods also produce a healthier food source. "There's scientific evidence to suggest that microgreens, and all plants, that are grown in soils under sunlight, have more nutritional value than those grown indoors," Jane says.

Supplying the local community with healthy, flavorful microgreens and edible flowers is not where it ends for Jane. "I don't want this to be just a microgreen and flower farm. I want to create a supported employment program," she says.

Through her past work, she has seen the incredible impact that farms and outdoor spaces can have on those with severe and persistent mental illnesses. "I saw the recovery. I saw them blossom and become completely different people," she says. "A farm creates such a therapeutic and relaxing environment that allows them to develop skills and confidence that bleed into other areas of their lives," she says.

"That is the big picture and 100 percent what I'm going to do," says Jane. It's a mission that brings the name of her farm full circle. Good Witch Farm. "Let's use our powers for good," she says.

Microgreen Smoothie

SERVES 1

When Jane of Good Witch Farm (page 232) told me how she uses her broccoli and pea microgreens, I immediately asked if she'd share the recipe for this book. It's simple and straightforward, and an easy way to get a boost of nutrients in the morning. You can also add it to your weekend brunch. "This is what healed me," she says of the recipe. Using her nutrient-rich microgreens like this is what healed her immune system after she was told it would never be the same again. The creamy smoothie is thin and easy to drink; if you like your smoothies on the thicker side like I do, use frozen blueberries.

½ cup broccoli microgreens

½ cup pea microgreens

1 cup blueberries

6 ounces coconut milk

Combine all the ingredients in a blender and puree for about 20 seconds, until smooth. Drink right away.

Good Witch Farm

Beach Picnic

SERVES 2+

This simple beach picnic is good for prepping ahead
of time so that you can pull it all together in your
picnic bag when you are ready to head to the water.
It's a combination of sandwiches with light snacks
that aren't too heavy for a warm day in the sunshine.

Dungeness Crab Sandwiches (page 199)
Green Garden Dip and Dressing (page 192) with
    fresh vegetables
Orange Salad (page 137)

SUGGESTED BEVERAGES

Hearst Ranch Winery, Paso Robles and San
    Simeon—Julia Rosé
Russian River Brewing Company STS Pils

Autumn Harvest Dinner

SERVES 4 WITH LEFTOVERS

This autumn-inspired dinner is ideal for a weekend meal or a holiday celebration. The recipes listed will feed four with leftovers. If you need to feed a larger table of guests, an easy way to do it is to add more sides. While the large pork chops serve four, with more sides you can slice the meat off the bone before serving and stretch the main course. You can also add a second main, such as Citrus Chicken (page 179), for those who may not prefer pork, or add a vegetarian option, such as the Coastal Roots' Mediterranean Stuffed Collard Greens (page 66).

Roasted Pork Chops with Red Grapes in Red
 Wine Gravy (page 187)
Hemly Pear Thanksgiving Dressing (page 126)
Rice and Kale Salad with Herb Vinaigrette
 and Parmesan (page 42)
Sweet Potato Dinner Rolls with Sage Brown
 Butter (page 72)
Sweet Potato Crumb Pie (page 76)

ADDITIONAL SIDES

Roasted Winter Squash with Onions and Blue
 Cheese (page 64)
Fuyu Persimmon Jicama Slaw (page 124)
Pomegranate Grain Salad with Walnuts
 (page 118)

SUGGESTED BEVERAGES

Dresser Winery, Paso Robles—Syrah
Theopolis Vineyards, Yorkville—Estate Grown
 Petite Sirah
Cultivar Wine, Napa Valley—Santa Lucia
 Highlands Pinot Noir

Citrus Honey Mai Tai

SERVES 4

I became well acquainted with Trader Vic's Mai Tai when we lived in Oakland, the city of its origin back in 1944. Aside from the cocktail itself being from California, I felt like an even stronger California farm–to–tiki mug twist was needed here. All the important flavors of the Mai Tai are present, but the drink uses a blend of citrus that has been lightly caramelized in a skillet. The honey syrup has a complex sweetness that complements the flavors of the citrus juice. I like using Sierra Honey Farm (page 94) honey in this cocktail, especially the Black Sage that Thomas accurately describes as having notes of fruit punch.

¼ cup honey

¼ cup water

8 small mandarins or tangerines

2 navel oranges

2 limes

1 lemon

4 ounces dark rum

4 ounces white rum

2 ounces orange curaçao

2 ounces orgeat syrup

1 ounce water

Fresh mint for garnish

Edible flowers for garnish

Note: You can use any mix of your favorite citrus fruits, you just need about 10 ounces of juice. Start by adding just 1 ounce of honey syrup. Then, add more to your preferred sweetness. I find 2 ounces gives it the right balance, but you should feel free to adjust it to your tastes. You can store any leftover syrup in the refrigerator for up to a week to use in other cocktails.

1. Combine the honey and water in a small saucepan and warm over medium-high heat. Stir 60 to 90 seconds until a syrup forms. Remove the pan from the burner and set aside.

2. Cut each citrus fruit in half. Heat a large non-stick skillet over medium-high. Work in batches and place the fruit, cut side down, in the skillet. Cook for 2 to 3 minutes, until the edges of the fruit begin to brown and caramelize. Transfer to a bowl and let sit until cool enough to handle.

3. Juice all the citrus halves. Transfer the juice to a quart-size jar with a lid.

4. Add the dark and white rum, orange curaçao, orgeat syrup, and water to the jar. Pour in 1 ounce of the honey syrup. Secure the lid and give the jar a few good shakes. Taste and add more honey syrup to reach your preferred sweetness.

5. Fill four 10- to 12-ounce cocktail glasses or tiki mugs with ice. Divide the cocktail among the glasses, pouring it over the ice. Slap the mint between your hands to release its oils. Garnish each cocktail with mint and an edible flower.

Happy Hour Hangout

SERVES 6 TO 8

This book is full of bites that would best be served hanging out with friends with a cocktail or beer in hand, but I've narrowed it down to three for this list. The dip can be made ahead of time and chilled before serving. The other two are best served warm soon after they are prepared.

Caramelized Onion Dip (page 56) with chips or crackers
Roasted Olives with Pearl Onions (page 112)
Beef and Bacon Cocktail Meatballs in Red Wine Glaze (164)

SUGGESTED BEVERAGES

Citrus Honey Mai Tai (page 238)
Grapefruit Fennel Martinez (page 242)
Sierra Nevada Brewing Company Pale Ale

GRAY WHALE GIN

JAN AND MARSH MOKHTARI, MANHATTAN BEACH

Jan and Marsh Mokhtari founded Golden State Distillery and created Gray Whale Gin for two reasons. The first, for family, their two daughters. Second, because ocean conservation is important to them. Their gin provides a way to support efforts that protect our oceans and sea life while celebrating the California coast. "Just by buying a bottle of Gray Whale Gin, you are supporting ocean conservation," says Marsh.

Through their partnership with Oceana and 1% for the Planet, they are spearheading significant legislative changes in fishing practices that reduce bycatch and preserve the ocean floor. They are making these changes in ways that ensure fishermen are compensated, limiting any negative impacts on their operations when they switch to more ocean-friendly fishing practices and the necessary gear.

Their gin is named for the 12,000-mile migration of the gray whale along California's coast between Mexico and the Arctic each year. During distillation, the gin is made with botanicals from six points around California. These include juniper from Big Sur, fir tree from Sonoma, mint from Santa Cruz, limes from the Temecula Valley, sea kelp from the Mendocino coast, and almonds from the Central Valley.

All these ingredients come together to create a crisp, aromatic gin with a flavor enhanced by the land that also hints at the ocean. "There's something refreshing about tasting your way along the coast," says Marsh.

Jan and Marsh believe that life is about the experience and enjoying this journey. Their gin provides a moment for enjoying the here and now with family and friends while also preserving the enjoyment of our environment and oceans for future generations.

Grapefruit Fennel Martinez

SERVES 1

According to the city of Martinez, California, the Martinez cocktail originated there in 1849 and eventually evolved into what we know today as a martini. Numerous recipes for the classic can be found online, but I knew a farm-to-table version had a place in this book. Specifically, one made with Gray Whale Gin, full of botanicals from the coastline of the state. I asked Jan and Marsh whether they had a recipe they'd be willing to share, and they went straight to Niki Kotantoulas, beverage director at Manuela in Los Angeles.

Niki says, "This is actually one of my dearest ways to drink gin. I very rarely order classics anymore, but I find this cocktail to be an exception. A classic Martinez is also one of my favorites to make at home. I've often experimented with culinary versions of it and this recipe is one of my favorites." She adds that it's fun to use different varieties of citrus, such as oro blanco or pomelo. Mixing and matching can lend the cocktail complex notes, but your standard grapefruit is just as lovely as well. The fennel gives this cocktail a touch of anise.

Niki's recipe for infusing the gin is for a full, 750 ml bottle of Gray Whale Gin, but if you'd like to save some of your bottle for other gin cocktails, I've experimented with cutting the infusion recipe in half with the same results.

1½ ounces infused Gray Whale Gin (recipe follows)

1½ ounces sweet vermouth

¼ ounce maraschino liqueur

2 dashes Angostura bitters

2 dashes Regan's No. 6 Orange Bitters

Grapefruit twist for garnish

Note: Niki infuses the gin using a sous vide method. If you don't have the equipment, you can follow the instructions using a one-gallon zip-top freezer bag as I did.

Combine the infused gin, sweet vermouth, maraschino liqueur, Angostura bitters, and orange bitters in a mixing glass with ice. Stir for about 30 revolutions. Strain into a coupe glass, garnish with the grapefruit twist, and serve.

GRAPEFRUIT FENNEL INFUSED GIN

MAKES ONE 750 ML BOTTLE

1 fennel bulb, chopped

Peel of 5 grapefruits

One 750 ml bottle Gray Whale Gin

1. Place the fennel and grapefruit peel in an airtight bag with the gin. I like to do a proper sous vide with this, but if you are lacking the equipment, you can achieve the same effect by gently heating enough water to submerge the bag in a medium pot on the stovetop over medium-high heat and bringing the water to approximately 136°F. Submerge your airtight bag for about an hour. After removing from the water, let the contents of the bag marinate for another 24 hours.

2. When it's time to strain, strain the grapefruit fennel gin through a fine strainer to remove all particles. Now, the gin is ready to mix.

Niki Kotantoulas
Beverage director, Manuela, for Gray Whale Gin

ACKNOWLEDGMENTS

I'd like to thank each and every farmer and grower, food and drink producer, fisherman, culinary professional, and researcher featured in this book. The fact that you welcomed me to your workplaces and homes and took the time to talk with me, walk with me, and cook with me is something I will forever be grateful for. Many of you shared and donated what you produce with me to help with the recipes in this book. Thank you. Thanks also to those who shared recipe ideas and who trusted me to publish their family recipes and original creations on these pages.

Thank you to fellow author and friend Karista Bennett, for your expertise and guidance in navigating the creation of this book. Thank you to friend Andrea Ratulowski, for cheering me on and for consulting on photo selections.

Thank you to all my recipe testers—Karista, Laura, Linda, Rita, Nicole, Corinne, Kristl, and Amy. Your care in preparation, thoughtful comments, and suggestions were essential in making the recipes in this book some of the best I have developed. Thanks to my agent, Leslie Stoker, for her expertise and guidance.

I've always been dumbfounded when I hear stories from other authors of the challenges faced when working with their publishers. I have none of those stories to share, as I've been fortunate to work with a team of people who exercise the utmost respect and are always open to my ideas. Thank you to Countryman Press—Ann, Isabel, Maya, and Allison—for being the best publishing team in the industry to work with and for giving me the opportunity to write and photograph this book.

RESOURCES

A

A Cook and Her Farmer—Oakland
Website: www.thecookandherfarmer
.com/

Admiral Maltings—Alameda
Website: admiralmaltings.com/

Apple Blossom Farms—Bonsall
Website: www.appleblossomfarms.co/

B

Berry Good Food Foundation
Website: berrygoodfood.org/

Big Sur Salts—Big Sur
Website: bigsursalts.com/

Blossom Bluff Orchards—Parlier
Website: www.blossombluff.com/

Bread Bike Bakery—San Luis Obispo
Website: www.slobreadbike.com/

Brown Girl Farms—Hayward
Website: browngirlfarms.com/

C

Capay Mills—Esparto
Website: www.capaymills.com/

Chef Christina Ng—San Diego
Chef Rachel Ponce—Paso Robles
Coastal Roots Farm—Encinitas
Website: coastalrootsfarm.org/

Commercial Fishermen of Santa Barbara
Website: www.cfsb.info/

Cultivar Wine—Napa Valley
Website: www.cultivarwine.com/

The Cultured Abalone Farm—
Santa Barbara
Website: culturedabalone.com/

D

Dresser Winery—Paso Robles
Website: www.dresserwinery.com/

F

FARMstead ED—San Luis Obispo
County
Website: farmsteaded.com/

Fishful Future—La Jolla
Website: www.fishfulfuture.com/

Fleurie Flower Studio—Reedley
Website: fleurieflower.com/

Foggy Bottoms Boys—Ferndale
Website: www.foggybottomsboys.com/

G

Get Hooked Seafood—Santa Barbara
Website: gethookedseafood.com/

Giovanni's Fish Market & Galley—
Morro Bay
Website: www.giosfish.com/

Good Witch Farm—Lompoc
Website: goodwitchfarm.com/

Gray Whale Gin—Manhattan Beach
Website: www.graywhalegin.com/

H

Hearst Ranch Winery—San Simeon
Website: www.hearstranchwinery.com/

Hemly Cider—Courtland
Website: www.hemlycider.com/

Hen and Harvest Farm—Turlock
Website: henandharvest.farm/

Hog Island Oyster Co.—Marshall
Website: hogislandoysters.com/

J

J. Marchini Farms—Le Grand
Website: jmarchinifarms.com/

K

Koda Farms—South Dos Palos
Website: www.kodafarms.com/

L

La Tourangelle Artisan Oils—Woodland
Website: latourangelle.com/

Lazy Arrow at Camatta Ranch—
Santa Margarita
Website: lazyarrowadventures.com/

Lumen Wines—Los Alamos
Website: www.lumenwines.com/

M

Masumoto Family Farm—Del Rey
Website: www.masumoto.com/

McKellar Family Farms, Farmer
Bob's World—Ivanhoe
Website: farmerbobsworld.com/

Moonstone Cellars—Cambria
Website: www.moonstonecellars.com/

N

National Oceanic and Atmospheric
Administration Southwest Fisheries
Science Center—La Jolla
Website: www.fisheries.noaa.gov/
    Website: about/southwest-fisheries
    -science-center

INDEX